THE VICTORIOUS EXPRESSION

HOWARD T. YOUNG

# The Victorious Expression

A Study of Four
Contemporary Spanish Poets

*Miguel de Unamuno*
*Antonio Machado*
*Juan Ramón Jiménez*
*Federico García Lorca*

*The University of Wisconsin Press*

Madison, 1964

Published by the University of Wisconsin Press
430 Sterling Court, Madison 6, Wisconsin


Copyright © 1964 by the Regents of the University of Wisconsin
Printed in the United States of America
by George Banta Company, Inc., Menasha, Wisconsin


Library of Congress Catalog Card Number 64–14508

# For Carol

"Mil gracias derramando"
St. John
of the Cross

Something of our emotions escapes us, something that is irreconcilable to logical symbols rationally articulated. At this barrier set up by the inability to equate the soul and the word, many pause. Though deeply moved, they do not know what to say. But in spite of all these difficulties, the poet—dissatisfied, perhaps, but still the supreme sayer—delivers to us at last his victorious expression.

Jorge Guillén,
*Language and Poetry: Some Poets of Spain*
(Cambridge, Mass: Harvard University Press, 1961), p. 151.

... la langue royale, faite pour la poésie.

Jean Cassou,
*Trois poètes: Rilke, Milosz, Machado*
(Paris: Plon, 1954), p. 93.

# PREFACE

Contemporary Spanish poetry is very slow in gaining the audience it deserves. There are rumors that a new Golden Age has been born in the Iberian Peninsula, and Gerald Brenan has quietly asserted that, after English, Spanish lyrics are the best in Europe. But these remain rumors and assertions that, despite a rash of translations here and in England, are largely unqualified and untested.

For the reader who would like to make the excursion into Castilian verse, a fresh lyric tone and deep native note wait. The present book seeks to facilitate his appreciation by offering translations, with commentary, of the works of four representative poets: Miguel de Unamuno, generally known in English only as an essayist and philosopher; Antonio Machado, the most revered of contemporary Spanish poets; Juan Ramón Jiménez, winner of the Nobel Prize for Literature in 1956; and Federico García Lorca, internationally famous since 1936 but worthy of still more attention.

I have not written a book for the specialist, although every serious reader is a specialist in a way, and certainly the person who picks up a book about foreign poetry displays a precise kind of curiosity. Nevertheless, I assume in the reader only an interest in poetry and a desire to learn more about a little-known area of European letters. A brief historical introduction will help him get his bearings for what lies ahead.

Many other poets are eminently worthy of consideration—

Pedro Salinas, Jorge Guillén, Rafael Alberti, Miguel Hernández, Luis Cernuda, Vicente Aleixandre, to name only a few. But Unamuno, Machado, Jiménez, and Lorca have been established to an extent that the others have not. These four embody most forcefully the principal themes and techniques of more than thirty years of Spanish poetry, and thus are decidedly worthy of being joined within the covers of a book devoted to the introduction of modern Spanish lyrics to a broader public.

During my work, I have had recourse to the labors of specialists, whom I acknowledge in the proper place. Their contributions have been especially valuable in clarifying various aspects of the men with whom we are dealing—Lorca's use of myth, for example, or Machado's debt to philosophy; but no study exists which we can cherish as the definitive presentation of any of the four poets in these pages. At the end of each section, I offer a list of original editions and a critical bibliography of the majority of existing English translations of Unamuno, Machado, Jiménez, and Lorca.

The mechanics of styling posed a thorny problem, that of differentiating between the ellipsis dots which indicate my own omissions and those employed by the poet as an integral part of the poem. This distinction had to be maintained, because Jiménez and Machado, in particular, were fond of leaving a sentence suspended in the air for the reader to fill in along lines suggested in the poem. If overworked, as in the case of Jiménez, the device is questionable, but, nevertheless, it is fairly common in all modern Spanish poets. The ellipsis dots which represent my own editorial paring have, therefore, been set with more space between them than those which the poet himself used as part of his poem. Hopefully, this is the least clumsy solution for a difficult technical problem. Throughout the Spanish text, I have followed the rules for spelling laid down by the Real Academia Española in 1959. Thus, *fue, fui, dio, vio,* which properly carried accents in my sources printed before the Academia ruling, here appear without them.

To translate poetry, it was declared at a Harvard symposium

on translation, another poem must be written. This may be true, but in the present case, it would presuppose a poet as well as a critic, an achievement the author cannot lay claim to. Furthermore, in the process of writing a new poem—or imitating one, as Robert Lowell calls it—the original bond between sound and sense is sundered. My efforts have been directed instead toward elucidating the magic relationship between word and meaning by means of a commentary on the poems which, it is hoped, will restore some of the enchantment lost in translation, and compensate for the restraint of my own versions. This restraint, however, has not bound me to a literal translation. Whenever possible without forcing or padding, I have refused the obvious connotation and tried to enhance the so-called true version. Lorca's "y se abría el azogue / de los espejos" may be rendered as "the quicksilver split / in the mirrors," avoiding the literal meaning of *abrirse* (to open) while retaining an assonance that is present in the original. In the case of a direct style like Machado's, the straightforward approach is usually the best. Instead of worrying "Tierra le dieron una tarde horrible," I have translated it directly as "Earth they gave him one horrible afternoon." In short, my criterion calls for a modest translation with only those liberties that the sound and rhythm of an English line demand. Gifted poet-translators can and have done more. Those readers who know Spanish will always realize how much is absent; those who do not may gain, at least, a glimpse of the "victorious expression."

Many persons helped me in the preparation of this book. For kind answers to nagging questions, I want to thank Eugenio Florit, A. Sánchez Barbudo, Manuel Durán, Charles Tomlinson, and Lucilo Escudero. Frederick Bracher cast a critical eye over sections of the manuscript and did his best to sharpen my prose. Hubert Herring and Leonard Pronko read the entire manuscript and were most helpful. I am grateful to the Honnold Library Research Fund for secretarial aid. Apart from the larger debt to my wife Carol, I owe her thanks for general

# CONTENTS

*Introduction*
*Antecedents and Attributes*
page xv

---

I

*Miguel de Unamuno*
1864–1936

*The Oldest Struggle*
page 1

---

II

*Antonio Machado*
1875–1939

*A Few True Words*
page 33

---

III

*Juan Ramón Jiménez*
1881–1958

*The Religion of Poetry*
page 75

---

IV

*Federico García Lorca*
1898–1936

*The Magic of Reality*
page 137

INDEX, page 217

# INTRODUCTION

## Antecedents and Attributes

Romanticism in Spain was on the whole an inferior imitation of English and French models that, imported from Paris, never developed native roots. In the Spanish character, the world and the ego were already locked together in passionate struggle, and the problem of salvation had been solved by the Church. Therefore, such images as we have of the poet suffering before the world, challenging beliefs, resisting storms, or wasting away for love derive from a deliberate Byronic pose. Spanish culture did not accord with romanticism, although, paradoxically, Spanish life appealed to Hugo, Southey, Byron, and Scott as romantic material.

An unfortunate legacy of the Romantic movement was rhetoricism. This tendency, already present in Spanish letters, was given lamentable stimulus by such a poet as Zorrilla, who cheerfully remarked that he had acquired the art of writing much and saying little. Poetry gained in length but not in sincerity. When romanticism waned, it was replaced by the hollow declamatory style of Núñez de Arce or the platitudes of Campoamor.

There are two remarkable exceptions in this nineteenth-century gallery of mediocrity. In Galicia, the Celtic, superstitious, rainy corner of Spain, a young woman began to write poems in the language of her province, paraphrasing the *cantigas de amigo,* traditional Galician-Portuguese love songs dating from

the thirteenth century. The voice of Rosalía de Castro (1837–
85) is like a pure bell, unsullied by the pretentious "official"
music of the period. Preoccupation with some private sorrow
marks nearly every line of poetry she wrote after her early love
lyrics, and her verse becomes, as does Emily Dickinson's, a series
of personal anecdotes presented in clear, uncluttered language.
Machado borrowed images from this "sad little Celtic woman,"
and Jiménez referred to her as "our Rosalía."

Gustavo Adolfo Bécquer (1836–70), bearing the fateful in-
heritance of his Nordic names, anticipated two chief concerns
of twentieth-century Spanish poets: the desire to express the
ineffable, and a keen awareness of the inadequacy of language.

Born in Seville, Bécquer lived a sickly life in Madrid and was
the victim of an unhappy marriage. At first glance, his *Rimas*
appear to be sad and sentimental love lyrics, and for this he
has been popular. But Bécquer walks the thin line between
valentine poetry and that of deep, simple emotion. What saves
him is his keen painter's eye. An image based on light often
leaps from the page to redeem an otherwise sentimental stanza.
The diffusion of light in nature created the harmony and deep
contentment of many of his finest poems.

Bécquer's ideas about writing provide a link between himself and modern Spanish poetry. He believed that the poet
united the world of form and the world of ideas through a
process of dreams. Bécquer, furthermore, was convinced that
words were inadequate in this rôle—they were wretched, clumsy
instruments, which the poet must always struggle to dominate.
But ideas, he said, were like butterflies: we try to grasp them,
and they flee, leaving only a trace of gold dust in our hands.

Rosalía de Castro and Bécquer broke with the conventional
modes of their time, and tried above all to be honestly themselves. Their sincerity makes them attractive today, but they
were little appreciated by their contemporaries. The case of
Rubén Darío (1867–1916) is quite different. This sensual His-
pano-Indian from Metapa, Nicaragua, issued a challenge to
poetry that made him famous. He proposed to renovate the

language, to introduce new themes and techniques (some of them no newer than the Middle Ages). From 1888 until the turn of the century, his ideas and his superb technical virtuosity produced ardent disciples and the usual handful of enemies wherever poetry was written in Spanish.

For Darío, the wind blew fair from France. The venerable Hugo taught him that extravagant emotion is not to be despised. The Parnassians offered a lesson in form and exotic themes. Verlaine showed him the power of suggestion and the importance of music. The resultant blending is known in Latin-American letters as *modernismo*.

The France of eighteenth-century Versailles, classical Greece, Leda and the swan, tales from China, the melancholy of princesses, sacred woods teeming with satyrs and nymphs—these were the subjects of Darío's verse. And he wrote about them with incomparable elegance, producing a poetry dependent upon the texture of objects and the delight of sound. His ideology was no more than could be expected from a hyper-aesthetic bohemian, but his poetic talent was unquestionable.

When Darío visited Spain for the second time, in 1899, he was no longer an obscure colonial but the recognized leader of a Latin-American literary movement beginning to exert an influence on the mother country. Among his first friends in Spain were Antonio Machado and Juan Ramón Jiménez. They had just discovered Verlaine and were eager to share their impressions with the stocky Nicaraguan, whose well-groomed hands and esoteric tastes belied his Indian features.

Darío's *modernismo* was new and exciting, but it did not long dominate the serious poets of Spain. The reason is that it ran headlong into a deeply ingrained tradition of sobriety. An analogy with painting may prove helpful. The large room devoted to Velázquez at the Prado produces an almost depressing sense of realism. Subdued browns, greys, and blues predominate. The effete faces of kings are surrounded by the lined countenances of peasants and dwarfs, by visages that reflect the tragedy of idiocy as well as the forcefulness of common people. With this tradition, Darío's swans and Aeolian lyres could have little compatibility; the nervous laughter of his French courtesans would find scarcely an echo in the grey austerity of central Spain. The somber Castilian heartland was incapable of embracing someone as exotic as Darío.

Unamuno was among the first to be annoyed by the "candied artificiality of the Nicaraguan." His reaction, though somewhat insular, is based on the accurate intuition that Darío was too uncomplicated and too foreign for the Castilian mind. For Unamuno, the spiritual lesson to be gained from developing native roots was more valuable than all the music from France.

Machado agreed with Unamuno. Jiménez was at first an eager convert to *modernismo,* but gradually and imperturbably worked toward his appointment with the absolute, an aspiration which he shares more closely with St. John of the Cross, Bécquer, and Valéry than with Darío.

Spain in 1898 had just undergone a sharply demoralizing experience, not calculated to make *modernismo* any more appealing, except as an escape. In a short period of months, she had lost the last of her once-great empire to the United States. The disaster of 1898 cut through the rhetoric that had drugged the country in the second half of the nineteenth century, and, in the words of the Basque writer Maeztu, revealed a fragile and bloodless body.

A group of men responded to the extremity of the Spanish condition with a sense of anguish. "Spain hurts me," cried Unamuno, setting the tone for a generation. Unamuno, Antonio Machado, the novelists Baroja and Azorín, and Maeztu reacted in varying ways and degrees to Spain's historical lag. They form the so-called Generation of '98, which launched the provocative enterprise of defining Spanish reality.

The temper of this generation overshadows *modernismo* and pervades the fibers of Spanish poetry in the first years of the new century. Even when they are not writing about Spain, these authors exhibit a sense of loss and melancholy that is part of the *Zeitgeist.* By the time of Lorca, nearly three decades later, the urgency felt by the Generation of '98 had diminished and *modernismo* had long since died. Lorca began under the influence of Machado and Jiménez. Later he took a brief look at surrealism, but he is essentially a product of Andalusian Spain, and foreign influences exerted very little change in his basic nature.

No background sketch of Spanish poetry is complete without mentioning the strong sense of tradition which continually sustains Spanish poets. Among the various roots of this tradition, the ballad form, called *romance* in Spanish, is the hardiest. It is a stanza of irregular length, composed of eight-syllable lines that alternately rhyme in assonance. Its monotonous measure was well-suited to the task of the minstrels, who used it to chant the deeds of national heroes. The steady and unpretentious rhythm, not unlike the strumming of a guitar, held the people's attention, as the troubadours sang of the Cid or of Count Fernán González, who fought for a free Castile.

For years, the *romances* were restricted to the popular expression of epic deeds and the reporting of incidents in the struggle between Christians and Moors. By 1550, literary men had collected and edited the ballads, and began to use them as models. Like a lodestone, the form has attracted nearly every Spanish poet, but it remained for twentieth-century poets to use the ballad stanza for the recording of subtle inner emotions. In the hands of Juan Ramón Jiménez, this sturdy popular mould became capable of containing extreme delicacies. In Lorca, it was expanded with virtuosity, warmth, and imagination. Antonio Machado, who employed the *romance* sparingly, nevertheless believed that it represented natural Spanish expression. For Unamuno, the *romance* spoke across ten centuries in tones both ancient and modern.

Literary movements from the rest of Europe have been absorbed by this tough and elastic form that serves as a vehicle for the soul of the Spanish people. If there is one common element among the poets in this book, it is their devotion to the *romance,* born under the sun of Castile and kept alive by a thousand voices.

The Spanish temperament is not merely a myth. Anyone who has lived in Spain will have remarked the rough edges of the people, their strident reaction to life's emergencies, the paradoxical amalgam of otherworldliness and emphasis on personal appearance, the dignity and pride of the individual. All these qualities impress themselves upon the outsider's mind and make him reluctant to accept the contention that national character does not exist.

A definition of the Iberian way of life must begin with its endemic tendency to personalize the world. Place a Spaniard in contact with another human being, an idea, or an object, and he will react with warm appreciation or hearty dislike. There will be no middle ground, and above all no objectivity. The result is an interesting, strongly individualistic community, bittersweet in its intensity. The *persona simpática* opens all doors because of his personal appeal. On the political level, the leader with a charismatic personality can easily overcome the talent of his opponents.

Other races probably react to life with equal intensity, but they have learned to sublimate their reactions or channel them into social and cultural activities. The result is a continuous level of civilization, such as that enjoyed by France. The Spaniard, on the other hand, is up and down. He is capable of furious activity when the goal is one he can wholeheartedly associate himself with, but he will fall into lassitude or bitter self-recrimination if he cannot find an ideal to which he is emotionally drawn. The energy of the Spanish nation blew like a gale across most of Europe and America in the sixteenth century as the kings pursued their ideal of a religiously united empire. Almost as abruptly as the passing of a storm, the *furia española* subsided in the following century.

The lyrical spontaneity of Spanish verse largely derives from this generous, sometimes extreme, subjectivity and emotionalism. In an age when European poets seem to have forgotten how to sing, the unabashed musical quality of Spanish poetry provides a pleasing exception. The strong presence of feeling has kept Spanish poets outside the gates of ideology through which many modern French and English poets have passed.

When the four poets in this book wrote about the poetic process, they were chiefly concerned with delineating the relationship between intellect and intuition, and fearful that the former would dominate. They felt that the intellect should guide expression, but the problem was always to keep the natural creative flow from being "sicklied o'er with the pale cast of thought." Lorca exemplifies a happy compromise: he was a great natural poet whose work is unencumbered with ideas; nevertheless, he was a careful craftsman who knew his limitations and worked with intellectual concern for words. The intellect, said Machado succinctly, has never sung, nor is song its mission. Spontaneity guided by intellect was Jiménez' formula for poetry; but, he said, when intelligence fails, feeling takes over. As for Unamuno, his whole life was a violent struggle against the domination of the intellect, which in poetry accounted for stilted verse and in philosophy created doubts about immortality.

One of the problems that has baffled poets in all languages is how to say the unsayable. The Spanish mind, with its strong mystic vein and generous emotional temperament, has long wrestled with the difficulties of describing the indescribable. St. John of the Cross, the chief mystic poet of Europe, settled for the partial expression of his unutterable rapture by means of symbols. Bécquer revived the task, and Jiménez devoted his life to it. Because of this transcendental urge, Spanish poets have been very conscious of the pressing contemporary concern in literature and philosophy with the use and meaning of words, the dismaying weakness of what T. S. Eliot called those "undisciplined squads of emotion" with which we make "a raid on the inarticulate."

The Spanish mind, and by extension the Latin mind, displays a marked visual sensitivity, a quick reaction to the form and beauty glistening in the Mediterranean atmosphere. As Ortega y Gasset pointed out, it is only in this sense that one may speak of Latin clarity. Even a writer like Cervantes, who resorted very little to description, caused Flaubert to exclaim: "Comme on voit ces routes d'Espagne qui ne sont nulle part décrites!" St. Ignatius de Loyola discerned this visual trait in his countrymen, and in the *Spiritual Exercises* stressed the need of a real image in order to promote fruitful meditation. The essayist Ganivet, echoing this need several centuries later, noted in 1897 in his *Idearium español* that an idea requires a visible form in order to be understood.

Lorca was, therefore, reacting to a long-felt necessity of Spaniards when he proclaimed sight as the principal human sense. As the world presses about to be recognized, the poet's duty is to see it for the first time. Each poem tries to re-create the initial glimpse of the Garden of Eden. Sometimes when the world became too magical or terrifying, Lorca turned to surrealism, but his keen visual sense always underscored the texture, line, and shape of real forms.

The other poets in this book react to reality in a visual way. The eye of Jiménez is basically impressionistic, seeking to capture the shifting, delicate nuances of light upon an object. In Machado's mind, the typical patio of Seville, like Proust's teacake, unlocked a flow of subjective association based on visual images. Later, in the Castilian plateau, Machado's eye still responded to traces of lavender and crimson color along the drab steppes. Only Unamuno seems relatively limited in his use of colors and not particularly concerned with visual effects in his poetry.

Intuitively, the Spanish poet personalizes the world and drinks in its beauty with his eyes. But he is always keenly aware that one day this deep-seated relationship between himself and his surroundings will be broken by death. Perhaps because beauty and the world mean so much to him, he is continually haunted and troubled by death. The average reader formed in the Anglo-Saxon tradition may even be put off by the continual presence of what Gide termed "lassitude and computation of death."

Depression and melancholy are, in part, the reverse of the

coin of involvement with the world. But every aspect of Spanish culture makes much of man's fate. The Spaniard, says Julián Marías, constantly thinks in terms of final things. This outlook makes him a basically religious individual, even though he may not accept the dogma of the church that rules his world. Being religious means that he broods in a way that the humanist or rationalist would not, on the insult of death.

But death, to use an ironic phrase of Marías, has never been granted citizenship in the United States. American readers may well discover in the intense Spanish involvement with man's mortality an instructive contrast with their own culture, which has yet to produce a sense of tragedy.

In Spanish literature, preoccupation with death has assumed two principal attitudes: one is stoical, with an underlying sense of anguish, as in Machado; the other is a fascinated revulsion that often is violently expressed, as in Lorca.

Tormented by an almost pathological fear of death, Jiménez managed to formulate a brave question: How can we fear death when it works constantly by our side? If it defines our existence, should we not accept it more readily? At any rate, no Spanish poet ever forgets its presence, and although he sometimes loses perspective and allows death to become an obsession, he is, on the whole, laboring to fulfill the intent of Rilke's observation: "Whoever rightly understands and celebrates death, at the same time magnifies life."

# I

# Miguel de Unamuno

## The Oldest Struggle

Why do they persist in making me into a
savant, a philosopher, or worse a politician?
No! I have never been more than a poet;
rather, nothing less than a poet.

Undated letter to Federico de Onís,
*La Torre,* IX,
Nos. 35–36 (1961), 59.

# These Confident Stones

The irascible Iberian that was Miguel de Unamuno is famous throughout Europe and America for his essays and novels, but very few people realize that he was also a poet who held the writing of poetry to be the highest form of human expression. Even in his own country, he is just now beginning to be accepted as one of the truly accomplished sonnet writers in the Spanish language. The irony would have amused Don Miguel, for he knew that his entire work was essentially poetic, and readily admitted that his antipathy toward systematic thought and his disgust with reason sprang from a feverishly imaginative mind, struggling to break the chains of literal language and objectivity.

The anguish that fills a thousand of Unamuno's pages can be summarized in one short sentence: Man's life is tragic because reason denies him the consolation of immortality. Holder of a chair in classics and later president of the University of Salamanca, he wrote about this tragedy of mankind, not as a philosopher and never as a professor, but as a poet, a man pouring his soul on paper. Like Kierkegaard, whom he greatly admired, he filled page after page with unsystematic insights; and like Kierkegaard, he recognized intelligence as the chief enemy, for intelligence would always insist that facts are facts: that man is born and dies, and there is no proof he is immortal.

Faced with the threat of oblivion, Unamuno reacted by exalting his uniquely intense character and, at the same time, by

4 Miguel de Unamuno

urging all men to shake off their lethargy and to suffer meaningfully, both individually and together. "Only common grief can sanctify us," one of his sonnets concludes (XIII, 607).[1] The man of flesh and bone, irrational, in love with life, must be the main topic of philosophy; otherwise, it is a mere exercise in abstract theory. In addition, every philosopher is more important than his philosophy.

To develop a system would be, in effect, to use intelligence against intelligence. Poetry—or, rather, the poetical method—was to be the chief weapon; paradox, contradiction, and emotion might scale the cold towers of reason. He waved aside all discussion of small points, and concentrated with exasperating bluntness on the main target: the tragedy of death. No solution was possible, but by battling daily against the inevitable, one acquired purpose, dignity, and a harsh consolation. Unamuno resolved to live each day as if it were his last, to pour himself so fully into each act that if, upon dying, he encountered *la nada* (nothingness), it would be a supreme insult. Such an attitude may be romantic, irrational, or silly—depending upon one's prejudice—but it is difficult to deny its poetic inspiration. "Among men," Unamuno wrote, "no one is greater than a lyric poet."[2]

His constant battle with death converted him into a twentieth-century Don Quixote—one who did not repent on his deathbed. When we criticize his stubbornness, his apparent folly, and his refusal to abandon the theme, we tend to forget one of the lessons Unamuno had obviously taken to heart from Kierkegaard: ". . . since the uncertainty [of death] is there in every moment, it can be overcome only by overcoming it in every moment."[3]

1. Unamuno's poetry is cited from Volumes XIII and XIV of *Obras completas,* ed. Manuel García Blanco (Madrid: Aguado, 1962, 1963), unless otherwise indicated. References are to volume and page. I should like to thank Fernando de Unamuno for permission to use these poems.
2. Quoted in Carlos Blanco Aguinaga, *Unamuno, teórico del lenguaje* (Mexico City: El Colegio de México, 1954), p. 91.
3. *Concluding Unscientific Postscript* (Princeton, N.J.: Princeton University Press, 1944), p. 149.

He began to write poetry rather late in life, around the age of thirty-five, and his first book of poems, called simply *Poesías,* did not appear until 1907. With considerable chagrin, he remarked that the best results of his pen "pass by houses but never enter in" (XIII, 887). While he was alive, he was rarely thought of as a poet, and, despite his reputation as a writer, none of his volumes of verse saw a second edition.[4]

Part of the reason that Unamuno's contemporaries failed to appreciate his poetry may be found in the literary tastes he cultivated. In an age that bowed to Verlaine and Mallarmé, he was fond of Tennyson, Carducci, Milton, and Dante. His training as a classical philologist oriented him toward the past, and his interest in religion made him a devoted reader of the Bible. When he was banished in 1924 to the tiny island of Fuerteventura in the Canaries, he took with him a copy of the New Testament in Greek, the *Divine Comedy,* and a volume of poems by Leopardi.[5] The subsequent "old-fashioned" note occasionally present in his poetry may be attributed to these personal preferences and to his dislike of literary trends. Furthermore, three of his most repeated themes, ancillary to the dominating motif, were family, religion, and *patria,* none of which was likely to arrest his contemporaries' attention. The publication of *The Christ of Velázquez (El Cristo de Velázquez)* in 1920 ran counter to two cherished axioms of the times: Long poems could not command an audience, and religious poetry was dead.[6]

To be out of step, however, was Unamuno's deliberate intention. He accented his idiosyncrasies, not only to arouse his readers from their lethargy, but also to call attention to himself and to secure the only kind of immortality that in his heart he knew to be possible, that of fame. Infamous or revered, Unamuno made certain that his presence was felt; he poured his

4. Manuel García Blanco, *Don Miguel de Unamuno y sus poesías* (Salamanca: University of Salamanca, 1954), p. 5.

5. *Ibid.,* p. 285.

6. Luis Cernuda, *Estudios sobre poesía española contemporánea* (Madrid: Guadarrama, 1957), p. 93.

spiritual anguish into every word, turning literature into a public confession, and in the end this conspicuous honesty made
him unique.

The conspiracy of silence against his poetry, for which he
was so largely responsible, has now been dissipated. Luis Cernuda, whose outlook could hardly be more different, recently
asserted that Unamuno was the major Spanish poet of this century and that his sonnets could stand alongside those of
Quevedo.[7]

Unamuno's first book of poetry (*Poesías,* 1907) contains a
forceful statement of his poetic creed. Partly as a reaction to
Rubén Darío and *modernismo,* the creed is strongly anti-aes-
thetic. Ideas—and, consequently, feelings, for in Unamuno the
two could never be separated—take precedence over all other
considerations. What the poet says is more important than how
he says it; meter, rhyme, and pattern are secondary to content
and emotion.

The poet is a sculptor, not a tailor. He is concerned with
tenuous things ("Let us carve the fog"), but he must keep his
expression rooted in the earth. Imagery threatens to disguise the
raw depths of emotion:

> ¿Imágenes? Estorban del lamento
> la desnudez profunda,
> ahogan en flores
> la solitaria nota honda y robusta...
> (XIII, 359)

> Images? They intrude upon grief's
> profound nakedness,
> and drown with flowers
> the robust, deep, and solitary note...

To Verlaine's famous injunction that music should be the
prime concern of a poet, Unamuno flatly replied, "Poetry . . . is
not music" (XIII, 200). Music is soothing; it heals wounds
(his senses) which he prefers to keep open toward infinity,
"bleeding with longing" (XIII, 394). Music lulls thought,

7. *Ibid.,* pp. 90, 93.

which he would rather have stamping in its stable like an imprisoned Pegasus. Thus his disdain for "this business called Art" (XIII, 850), simply another way of dissembling the tragic sense of life and turning poetry into a trivial exercise in decoration.

Unamuno tended to belabor his poetic credo, and when he closely applied its principles, the result was usually questionable, inelegant verse. But whether or not his ideas guaranteed good poetry, they did counterbalance the influence of *modernismo,* and would not go unheeded by his contemporaries. Write densely with few words, he says in his *Poesías* (XIII, 202), advice which became, as we shall see, the motto of Antonio Machado.

Even within the confines of the sonnet form, his brusque nature burst through. His sonnets have proper rhymes and observe the rules, but their content and inner rhythm are irregular, with the result that reading them is like riding along a bumpy road through a pleasantly landscaped countryside. In some cases, Unamuno simply neglected to polish his first draft. He was very fond of difficult and tortuous word order, and repeated phrases carelessly, although sometimes for effect. Paradoxes are plentiful because they jar the reader into fuller participation: ". . . lull / this suffering so that thus I may attain / the continual suffering of it" (XIII, 258). Strident consonance is used in the heat of creation and never softened in rewriting, even though it may be in contradiction to the idea Unamuno is seeking to portray: ". . . la callada vida / acurrucada en recatado olvido" (". . . the quiet life / crouched in concealed forgetfulness") (XIII, 274).

Language should be harsh and crude, pelting the reader with words so as to rouse him from indifference, the unforgivable sin in Unamuno's religion. *Fábrica* (factory), *escarbar* (to scrape), *crujir* (to crackle), *triturar* (to crush), *cuajarón* (clot), *horrura* (filth), *costra* (scab), and *desollar* (to flay) are among words he is addicted to using in his first books of poetry.

Alongside these inelegant notes, one discovers with pleasant surprise the Miltonic flow of *The Christ of Velázquez,* and the subdued sadness of his later sonnets. Thus the contradiction of his life persisted in his style.

The exaltation of Castile, the heartland of Spain, begins in Unamuno and becomes consequently a dominant theme of contemporary Spanish literature. The rugged, hard landscape of this section of Spain provided a perfect complement to the kind of poetry he advocated. While Darío worried about sad princesses and the enigma of the swan's neck, Unamuno offered the seared soil of Castile as the substance of verse.

The untutored foreigner tends to think of Spain in terms of indolent guitar music and orange trees, gypsy wailings and carnation-crowned *señoritas*. He has not looked closely enough at Goya and Velázquez, for Spain is a somber country, where the struggle for existence has been sharp. The key to understanding Spain and its essential meaning Unamuno felt to be in Castile, the uncomfortable, arid, windswept plateau which, as Alonso Fernández Coronel observed before the ax fell on his neck, creates men and then undoes them. In one of his most celebrated poems, the first two stanzas of which follow, Unamuno pictured Castile as a land that raises and invigorates the human spirit, exposing it to a sense of tradition and eternity:

> Tú me levantas, tierra de Castilla,
> en la rugosa palma de tu mano,
> al cielo que te enciende y te refresca,
>     al cielo, tu amo.
>
> Tierra nervuda, enjuta, despejada,
> madre de corazones y de brazos,
> toma el presente en ti viejos colores
>     del noble antaño.
>
>                   (XIII, 213)

> You lift me up, land of Castile,
> in the wrinkled palm of your hand,
> to the sky that kindles and cools,
>     to the sky, your master.
>
> Vigorous, lean, and open land,
> mother of stout-hearted men,

> from you the present takes the ancient colors
> of a noble past.

Castilian terrain has been scarred by the upheavals of nature; huge boulders lie flung about as if at the whim of some Iberian giant. Unamuno, quick to appreciate the stern scene, fashioned from it one of the key symbols of his poetry: *las piedras* (stones). These stones, of a particular yellow color in Salamanca where he spent most of his life, were prominently present in the construction of the university and cathedral. In the lengthy poem "Salamanca,"[8] we can see the paradoxical comfort he drew from their cold, hard nature:

> Alto soto de torres que al ponerse
> tras las encinas que el celaje esmaltan
> dora a los rayos de su lumbre el padre
>     sol de Castilla;
>
> bosque de piedras que arrancó la historia
> a las entrañas de la tierra madre,
> remanso de quietud, yo te bendigo,
>     ¡mi Salamanca!
>
> Miras a un lado, allende el Tormes lento,
> de las encinas el follaje pardo
> cual el follaje de tu piedra, inmoble,
>     denso y perenne.
>
> Y de otro lado, por la calva Armuña,
> ondea el trigo, cual tu piedra, de oro,
> y entre los surcos al morir la tarde
>     duerme el sosiego.
>
> Duerme el sosiego, la esperanza duerme,
> de otras cosechas y otras dulces tardes,
> las horas al correr sobre la tierra
>     dejan su rastro.
>
> Al pie de tus sillares, Salamanca,
> de las cosechas del pensar tranquilo
> que año tras año maduró tus aulas,
>     duerme el recuerdo.

8. The original poem consists of thirty-one stanzas. I have omitted sections referring to local landmarks at the University of Salamanca and to the students' emotional life, for these parts seem supplementary to the main themes of stone and eternity.

Duerme el recuerdo, la esperanza duerme,
y es el tranquilo curso de tu vida
como el crecer de las encinas, lento,
       lento y seguro.

De entre tus piedras seculares, tumba
de remembranzas del ayer glorioso,
de entre tus piedras recogió mi espíritu
       fe, paz y fuerza.

.   .   .   .   .   .   .   .   .   .

Sueño de no morir es el que infundes
a los que beben de tu dulce calma,
sueño de no morir ese que dicen
       culto a la muerte.

.   .   .   .   .   .   .   .   .   .

Pedernoso cual tú sea mi nombre
de los tiempos la roña resistiendo,
y por encima al tráfago del mundo
       resuene limpio.

Pregona eternidad tu alma de piedra
y amor de vida en tu regazo arraiga,
amor de vida eterna, y a su sombra
       amor de amores.

.   .   .   .   .   .   .   .   .   .

Y cuando el sol al acostarse encienda
el oro secular que te recama,
con tu lenguaje, de lo eterno heraldo,
       di tú que he sido.

                    (XIII, 216–20)

High thicket of towers turned to gold
by rays of the patriarch sun of Castile,
setting behind oaks that embellish
       the shifting sky;

stony forest that history tore
from the bowels of mother earth,
silent backwater, I bless you,
       my Salamanca!

From one side you see, beyond the slow Tormes,
the dusky foliage of oaks,
like the foliage of your stone, unmovable,
       dense, and perennial.

On the other side, by bare Armuña,
the wheat ruffles like golden stone,
and between the furrows of dying day
　　　serenity dreams.

Serenity dreams, and with it expectation;
while of past harvests and other gentle afternoons
the hours, racing over the earth,
　　　leave a trace.

At the foot of your hewn stone, Salamanca,
of the harvest of tranquil thought,
ripened each year in your halls,
　　　memory dreams.

Memory dreams, and with it expectation;
the tranquil course of your life
is like the growing of your oaks, slow,
　　　slow, and certain.

From your ageless rocks, tomb
of memories' glorious yesterdays,
from among your rocks my spirit gathered
　　　faith, peace, and strength.

.　　.　　.　　.　　.　　.　　.　　.　　.

The dream of never dying you infuse
in those who drink your gentle calm,
that dream of never dying they call
　　　the cult of death.

.　　.　　.　　.　　.　　.　　.　　.　　.

Rocky like you let my name be,
resisting the rust of time,
above life's drudgery
　　　resounding clear.

Your soul of stone proclaims eternity,
and love of life takes root in your lap,
love of eternal life, and in its shadow
　　　the love of loves.

.　　.　　.　　.　　.　　.　　.　　.　　.

As the reclining sun kindles
your ancient golden border,
say by the eternal herald of your tongue
　　　that I once was.

In spite of the efforts to evoke serenity, "Salamanca" does not strike the reader as a gentle composition. The metaphors of stone jut forth from the golden haze surrounding the university town and serve as a reminder of the poem's rugged basis. Unamuno constantly referred to images of stone in his early discussions of poetry; he saw the poet as a sculptor moulding his work to the contours of earth, and he hoped that his own verse would fasten itself "in the rocky recess of eternity" (XIII, 198). Among the rocks of Salamanca, he was quick to remark a strange sort of tranquillity. The symbol of endurance and re-sistance is clear enough, but it is harshly paradoxical to expand the concept to include a love of life discovered in the lap of stone and to receive from lifeless boulders intimations of im-mortality. Yet this was exactly the kind of stringent qualifica-tion that kept comfort from becoming conformity. Unamuno may have had in mind the biblical image of the Church founded upon the rock, for he mentions in another poem that when, as a youth, he entered the Basilica of Bilbao, he first felt the need for certainty under its "confident stones" (XIII, 255).

Unamuno's characteristic fondness for paradox urged him to build a song out of bare rock. In this grave stone land, he knew a forbidding "gothic calm" that possibly strengthened him for his struggle with death, his favorite adversary.

# The Denial of Peace

The man was on the point of being a monomaniac; he found evidence of mortality in everything he saw or did. He was afraid the obsession lurked in his eyes for his children to see. The crude, naturalistic figure of a reclining Christ in Palencia provoked the old horror: "This Christ immortal as death / will not rise up again; what for? nothing awaits / except death itself" (XIII, 839–40). Vengefully, he described in detail the twisted physical features of the figure, underlining its mortality, and, in doing so, emphasizing the mortality of the Resurrection legend. New Year's Eve, 1906, a sense of death pressed about him closely from the shadows of his study and drove him feverishly to complete a poem he was writing. Its last line read triumphantly, "I am finished and still alive!" (XIII, 435).

Clearly, no individual can remain within the limits of sanity and support such a febrile awareness of death, and the agonistic Unamuno, who seemingly suffered every second, was, in part, a self-created legend. At hand was a ready comfort, the age-old release found in the contemplation of nature. To stand on a hillside and feel oneself part of "earth's diurnal course" is to sense the continuity of life, to feel the urge to submit peacefully to the unconscious and stately rhythm of time. Many of these tranquil moments coexist with the bellicose cries of Unamuno the warrior, although frequently they are never more than a brief, almost guilty respite, which he takes care to contradict at the end of a sonnet:

> Pasaron como pasan por la cumbre
> rezagadas las nubes del estío
> sin dejar en los riscos el rocío
> de sus pechos; pasaron, y la lumbre
>
> del sol, desenvainada, pesadumbre
> para su frente fue; lejos, el río,
> por la fronda velado, a mi desvío
> cantando reclamaba a la costumbre.
>
> De la montaña al pie verdeaba el valle
> del sosiego en eterna primavera,
> rompía entre sus árboles la calle
>
> pedregosa que sube a la cantera,
> y en el delirio el susurrar del dalle
> de la muerte segando en la ribera.
> (XIII, 511)

> They passed as usual over the peaks,
> the straggling summer clouds,
> their breasts withholding rain
> from the crags; they passed, and light
>
> unsheathed by the sun was heavy
> upon their foreheads; afar the river,

in verdure veiled, to my indifference
called with its customary song.

Between mountains, the serene valley
turned green in timeless spring;
from out of trees the road broke,

mounting its rocky way to the stone quarry;
and in the rapture, the whispering sickle
of death mowed along the river.

Nothing prepares us for the final two lines. They intrude upon
a description of nature with the troublesome reminder that
above all such scenes stands the eternal reaper. The whispering
of the wind through the tall grass is a song for our death. Many
poems in *Rosary of Lyric Sonnets* (*Rosario de sonetos líricos,*
1912) begin in response to a movement of evening light or an
arresting cloud formation, but close with a metaphor of death
that reproves both the reader and Unamuno for forgetting their
mortality by surrendering to the beauty of the world, a world
which will soon betray them as part of its implacable system.

Yet occasionally this irascible rebel against human fate did
succumb to the desire for peace, for there also existed the man
who has been called the "contemplative Unamuno."[9] Striving
for recognition amidst the tocsins of war were the warm memories of his youthful home in Bilbao, the influence of his
mother, and the genuine love and maternal comfort he drew
from his wife. In 1895, in an essay on Spanish history, he insisted that the harmonious arrangement of the world was re-
flected in man's ability to sense peace, and that struggle was
not the law of life. The hero of his first novel *Peace in War*
(*Paz en la guerra,* 1897) had a vision of the deep silence, the
eternal quietness beneath all passing agitation, which inspired
the book's title. Shortly after 1900, Unamuno began to destroy
this vision, savagely suppressing his longing to blend into the
impersonal plan of the universe. Yet many instances in his
poetry demonstrate that the desire was always present and that
the "deepest doctrine" of life might be found in surrender:

9. Carlos Blanco Aguinaga, *El Unamuno contemplativo* (Mexico City: El
Colegio de México, 1959), convincingly demonstrates that all is not war,
anguish, and fear of death in Unamuno.

Junto a la laguna del Cristo
en la aldehuela de Yeltes,
una noche de luna llena

Noche blanca en que el agua cristalina
duerme queda en su lecho de laguna
sobre la cual redonda llena luna
que ejército de estrellas encamina

vela, y se espeja una redonda encina
en el espejo sin rizada alguna;
noche blanca en que el agua hace de cuna
de la más alta y más honda doctrina.

Es un rasgón del cielo que abrazado
tiene en sus brazos la Naturaleza;
es un rasgón del cielo que ha posado

y en el silencio de la noche reza
la oración del amante resignado
sólo al amor, que es su única riqueza.

(XIII, 577)

Beside the Lagoon of Christ
in the hamlet of Yeltes
on a night of full moon

White night in which the transparent water
quietly sleeps in the bed of its lagoon,
while overhead the full, round moon
escorts an army of stars

and sets its watch; a round oak clearly shines
in the mirror untouched by a single ripple;
white night in which the water becomes a cradle
for the highest and deepest doctrine.

The water is a shred of sky
enfolded in nature's arms;
a shred of sky that has come to rest,

and amidst the silent night repeats
the prayer of a lover resigned
to the riches of love alone.

In reality, however, these thoughtful, pensive moments always
had contrary sides, for when pain grows silent, death is heard,
and the peace that he found in the breast of unconsciousness

was, from the point of view of the *agonista,* a fraud. The vituperative combatant and the lover of nature's serene order join together to enhance the complexity of Unamuno's character. Unless we perceive the interaction of one upon the other, we are left with the lopsided impression of a Spanish professor shaking his fist at the sky. During the years of his exile, which began in 1924, he met again, as we shall see, the temptation to yield, this time to the maternal arms of the sea.

It is well to emphasize the little-known contemplative vein of Unamuno's character, for it has been overshadowed by the figure of the fierce and tireless warrior. The reason that caused Unamuno to suppress the tendency of his spirit to seek release in a kind of pantheism may be traced, at least in part, to a religious crisis he suffered in the closing years of the century.[10] His omnivorous reading and keen intelligence had weakened the candid belief of his boyhood, a belief that had been unusually fervid and which contained all the symptoms of a mystic *manqué.* When he was unable to sustain this deep and passionate faith in the face of what his vast reading had taught him, he experienced several violent, almost pathological, seizures, during which he retreated to a monastery to think and to pray. Out of these crises, he developed the dominant convictions of his later life: to struggle for the sake of struggle, to believe in the need to believe, even if he himself could not believe. His paradoxes symbolize a lasting insecurity. To argue whether or not Unamuno ever really regained his faith is not our task, but we may assert that the cause of the contradiction and agony of his work is due to the lost illusion to which he poignantly refers:

> En la sombra la lluvia se diluye
> y en el silencio el son de la campana,
> nocturno el río de las horas fluye
>
> desde su manantial, que es el mañana
> eterno, y en sus negras aguas huye
> aquella mi ilusión harto temprana.
>
> (XIII, 594)

10. Antonio Sánchez Barbudo, *Estudios sobre Unamuno y Machado* (Madrid: Guadarrama, 1959), explores the religious crisis of Unamuno's life.

The rain dissolves in shadow
and silence dilutes the bell's sound;
the night river of time flows

from its fountainhead, the eternal
tomorrow, and in its black waters
flees my premature illusion.

Along with illusion fled the hope for life after death, and it should not be forgotten that Unamuno's conception of immortality was, for modern theologians at least, shockingly unsophisticated. Immortality meant the continuance of Don Miguel de Unamuno as he now existed in a given year in Salamanca, Spain. A platonic heaven of ideas horrified him:

¡El otro mundo es el del puro espíritu!
¡Del espíritu puro!
¡Oh, terrible pureza,
inanidad, vacío!

(XIII, 350)

The other world is of pure spirit!
Pure spirit!
Oh, terrible purity,
inane, empty!

# The Struggle

Resisting the normal impulse of the weary man to rest and entertaining no thought of victory, Unamuno declared war on man's fate. "My religion is to seek truth in life and life in truth, knowing full well that I shall never find them while I live. My religion is to struggle incessantly and tirelessly with the unknown. My religion is to wrestle with God from break of day until nightfall, as Jacob was supposed to have done. I cannot give in to the idea of the unknowable. . . . I reject the eternal *ignorabimus*. . . . I shall spend my life struggling with the unknown, because this struggle is my sustenance and my comfort."[11]

11. *Mi religión y otros ensayos,* 2nd ed. (Buenos Aires: Espasa-Calpe, 1945), pp. 10, 12.

These famous words were written the year that *Poesías* was published. In his first poems, he makes it quite clear that this struggle, "without hatred and without softness" (XIII, 270), is carried on by means of poetry:

> ... de paz el día
> si es dulce, es porque hacemos en su seno
> con la pasada guerra poesía.
> (XIII, 570)

> ... if the peace of day
> is sweet, it is because in its breast
> we make poetry from recent war.

Struggle was an affirmation of himself, a vital projection of his personality. As a warrior gains glory and renown in battle, Unamuno sought, through strife, to realize his personality in its fullest measure, and, in the process, to achieve the real immortality of fame. His controversial interpretation of Don Quixote (*The Life of Don Quixote and Sancho,* 1905) is based on this premise. Unamuno was tantalized by the fact that Don Quixote honestly proclaimed his desire for fame. The lean knight had set out from his village in La Mancha to undo wrongs, succor the needy, and earn the glorious acclaim of the world. Straightforward and unwavering in his purpose, Don Quixote became in the eyes of Unamuno a prophet, a divinely inspired figure preaching the doctrine of quixotism, which is the doctrine of immortality through mundane glory, salvation through high-minded battle against the mean reality of the world. Turning Cervantine irony into the tragic irony of life, Unamuno exalted Don Quixote as a stirring figure struggling against human fate. When critics objected, Unamuno reiterated his basic position: that each individual must interpret a work of art, a book, or a philosophy in terms of his own vital needs and desires.

Unamuno's continual advocacy of struggle as a way of life throws light on the thorny, egotistical side of his character, which was the despair of his friends. As an agonist—an actor in conflict with destiny and fellow men—Unamuno conceived of his friends and his public as adversaries. He wrote or spoke against someone or something, and nearly all of his essays begin with a reference to a specific individual. Nothing escaped his displeasure or his quick shifts of opinion. When his fellow Basques invited him to speak, he badgered them about their nationalism and suggested that they bury their language. He denounced the military, and when delighted politicians asked to hear him, he delivered a sharp criticism of politics. From one point of view, these actions may be dismissed as merely cantankerous. But in a deeper sense, they represent his refusal to restrict his personality by adhering to any group or party. "No soy un partido, soy un todo," he was fond of saying: "I am not a part, I am a whole."

When the Republic was established, he became its sharp critic. Spain is a republic with twenty million kings, he remarked, putting his finger on the basic Spanish problem—lack of social cohesion. His first response to the Franco uprising was favorable, but he soon turned against the Fascists, and in a remarkable speech at Salamanca told the angry partisans of reaction in his audience: "You will conquer, but you will not convince." As a result, he was confined to his house. A remark to a visiting foreigner revealed the true nature of his character: "I shall never be with the conqueror!"[12] He died shortly afterwards, and it is easy to believe that, shut up in his house, his voice extinguished itself because it could not speak. His antagonist had been taken from him, and consequently the source of his immortality.

For someone who viewed life as a conflict, dogmatic faith—untested, unquestioning—was merely a living death. Unamuno wanted to believe, and he passionately proclaimed the necessity for belief. But he was certain, as had been Pascal, that faith could not exist without doubt:

> La vida es duda,
> y la fe sin la duda es sólo muerte.

.     .     .     .     .     .

12. Federico de Onís, "Unamuno íntimo," in *España en América* (Río Piedras: University of Puerto Rico, 1955), pp. 435–36, 440.

pues sólo es tuyo
quien confiese, Señor, no conocerte.

.     .     .     .     .     .     .     .

Yo te siento, Señor, no te conozco, . . .
(XIII, 287)

Life is doubt,
and faith without doubt is only death.

.     .     .     .     .     .     .     .

only he is yours,
O Lord, who confesses he knows you not.

.     .     .     .     .     .     .     .

I feel you, Lord, I do not know you, . . .

Beyond this statement of faith, Unamuno refused to go, and there are grounds for believing that he had even less faith than this. He preferred to impose upon his readers the tension created by feeling God but not rationally knowing him, so that they too would grapple daily with doubt and attain a more authentic existence.[13]

The ideas concerning God that spring from this battling, doubting faith have aligned Unamuno quite closely with certain existentialists. He believed that man created God in order to be assured of eternal life. Without that promise, God was unnecessary. Man's existence defines the essence of God, a truly heretical thought in Spain, and one with which Sartre could find little quarrel. In the widely translated novel *Mist* (*Niebla,* 1914), Unamuno played with the relation between God and man by putting it into the artistic terms of a creator and his creations. Do the characters brought into being by an author have any life of their own? In *Mist,* the chief character invades Unamuno's study to argue this question, a device which anticipates Pirandello's *Six Characters in Search of an Author.* In 1907, the problem had been expressed in poetry:

13. His ideas are contradictory enough to allow opposing interpretations. So eminent a critic as Julián Marías believes that when Unamuno is stripped of deliberate contradictions, his orthodoxy shines through; see *Miguel de Unamuno* (Madrid: Espasa-Calpe, 1943). Sánchez Barbudo, *Unamuno y Machado,* contends that Unamuno never acquired faith and chides him for obfuscating the issue with such phrases as "I believe that I believe."

¿Dónde estás, mi Señor; acaso existes?
¿Eres tú creación de mi congoja,
o lo soy tuya?

.    .    .    .    .    .    .    .    .

¿Tú, Señor, nos hiciste
para que a ti te hagamos,
o es que te hacemos
para que Tú nos hagas?

.    .    .    .    .    .    .    .    .

Tú me abrirás la puerta cuando muera,
la puerta de la muerte,
y entonces la verdad veré de lleno,
sabré si Tú eres
o dormiré en tu tumba.

(XIII, 281–85)

Where art thou, my Lord, dost thou indeed exist?
Art thou creation of my anguish,
or am I thine?

.    .    .    .    .    .    .    .    .

Hast thou, Lord, made us
so that we may make thee,
or do we make thee
so that thou mayest fashion us?

.    .    .    .    .    .    .    .    .

Thou shalt open the door when I die,
the door of death,
and then I shall see the truth in full.
I shall know if thou art,
or I shall sleep in thy tomb.

If death is absolute, both God and Unamuno die together, a position foreshadowed long ago in these lines from the seventeenth-century German mystic Angelus Silesius: "I know, deprived of me, / God could not live a wink. / He must give up the ghost / If into naught I sink."[14]

Underneath the apparent heterodoxy and the agonized rebellion lay the basic heritage and training of a Roman Catholic. This fact may be appreciated in *The Christ of Velázquez.* Over

14. *A Selection from the Rhymes of a German Mystic,* trans. Paul Carus (Chicago: The Open Court Publishing Co., 1909), p. 15.

a considerable period of time he read to his friends bits of a
poem to which he had devoted painstaking care, rewriting more
than he was accustomed to. When it finally appeared, it was a
masterpiece of religious poetry, baroque in its density and tension, strongly human in its evocation of the crucified Lord, and,
in its sensuous, pictorial effect, symptomatic of the Latin Catholic upbringing of its author.

The Velázquez Christ, notable for its tranquillity and tenderness, is not always a favorite among the mass of Spanish Catholics, who prefer their crucifixion to be more agonizing. But for
Unamuno, it was immensely attractive—the figure of God in a
most human form—and he celebrated all aspects of the Velázquez painting in eighty-five sections of blank verse, interwoven
with hundreds of biblical citations and presented in a verse-para-
graph form reminiscent of Milton.[15]

The strong natural presentation of Christ's body in the painting, and especially its manliness, impressed Unamuno:

> . . . es todo un hombre el Dios de nuestra noche
> y hombría es su humanidad divina.
>                                         (XIII, 660)

> . . . the God of our night is every inch a man,
> and manliness is his divine humanity.

Although manliness here has virile connotations, it underlines,
in addition, the figure's brotherhood to all mankind.

The painting also possesses a luminous quality, offset by a dark
background. Unamuno seized upon this divine chiaroscuro as
the basis for the symbolism of the first part of his poem:

> Blanco tu cuerpo está como el espejo
> del padre de la luz, del sol vivífico;
> blanco tu cuerpo al modo de la luna
> que muerta ronda en torno de su madre
> nuestra cansada vagabunda tierra;
> blanco tu cuerpo está como la hostia
> del cielo de la noche soberana,

15. Calvin Cannon, "The Miltonic Rhythm of Unamuno's *El Cristo de
Velázquez,*" *Hispania,* XLIV (1961), 95–98.

de ese cielo tan negro como el velo
de tu abundosa cabellera negra
de nazareno.

(XIII, 655–56)

White is your body like the mirror
of the father of light, the life-giving sun;
white is your body as the moon,
circling in death round its mother,
our tired vagabond earth;
white is your body like the host
of the sky in the sovereign night
of heaven, black as the veil
of your dark, abundant
Nazarene locks.

The moon is Christ, the sun is God, and the earth is Mary. Sketches in his study at Salamanca attest to this basic symbolism of the poem.[16] Out of the uncanny whiteness of the Velázquez original has been spun a literal ray of hope, for light equals life in any language and in any symbolism, and Christ reflects the light of God. Upon "a snowstorm of light," Unamuno erected a shimmering, luminescent tower that aspired to eternity.

All parts of the scene are described in detail, from the crown of thorns to the earth upon which the cross rests; from the index finger of the right hand to the groin and knees—all done in frankness, love, and humanity.

It is a great religious poem, orthodox (unless one digs too deeply into the atavistic connotations of the symbols), baroque, impassioned, and worthy of comparison with the best religious lyrics of the *Siglo de oro*. Theme and vitality were for once completely in harmony in Unamuno.

16. Calvin Cannon, "The Mythic Cosmology of Unamuno's *El Cristo de Velázquez*," *Hispanic Review*, XXVIII (1960), 28–39. "The sun, the moon, and the earth, each in its mythic significance [as Jungian archetypes] is the eternal and primordial assurance that death is not absolute" (pp. 38–39). Along similar lines, Juan Ramón Jiménez has pointed out that *El Cristo de Velázquez* is essentially a book of mythology, and also accurately notes that it is the only sensual work by Unamuno, whose attitude toward voluptuousness coincided more with Protestant ethics than with those of Latin Catholics. See Ricardo Gullón, *Conversaciones con Juan Ramón* (Madrid: Taurus, 1958), pp. 71–72.

# Exile and the Sea

When Unamuno carried into the arena of politics the unceasing criticism and constant asperity that moulded his combative vision of life, he found himself *persona non grata* in his own country. The mild little dictator Primo de Rivera felt called upon to banish him to the Canary Island of Fuerteventura in 1924. An international uproar ensued, for Unamuno had won the fame dear to his heart, and the embarrassed dictator made it easy for the gadfly professor of classics to escape to Paris. There Unamuno roamed unhappily about, gathering with fellow Spaniards every afternoon at the café La Rotonde, and writing a great deal of poetry. Finally he settled in Hendaye, from whence each day his eyes could gaze upon the mountains of Spain. Poetry had become his great solace. *From Fuerteventura to Paris* (*De Fuerteventura a París,* 1925); a series of splendid sonnets, *Ballads in Exile* (*Romancero del destierro,* 1927); and the first part of his *Song Book* (*Cancionero*), published posthumously in 1953, are the products of these uprooted years.

Exile affected Unamuno profoundly. When he returned to Spain after six years, his hair and beard were white. But the greatest testimony of change lies in his poetry. Removed from his antagonist, set aside from the struggle, although partially continuing it in conversation and scores of newspaper articles, he found, against his will, time for quiet contemplation. The vision of peace that he had had as a youth in the Basque country and expressed as the thesis of his first novel returned in the massive presence of the sea. And, although he continued to recognize the ambiguous nature of rest and thought of it uneasily as a rehearsal for death, he ceased trying to smother his tendency to accept stillness. With rare melancholy, a poignant sense of age crept into his work. And he returned to the sonnet form. His pugnacious rejection of form in *Poesías* had, as we have said, been partially inspired by his dislike of *modernismo.* In reality, his frenetic, restless creativity greatly needed a mould. Hence, it is not surprising that within the confines of the sonnet he could write his greatest poetry.

During the first weeks in Fuerteventura, he metaphorically plunged into the sea, embracing it as he would a wife (XIV, 508). The anecdotal aspect of the seaside, with its fishermen and ships, does not appear, but only the sea itself in a mystical vision:

> . . . el alma siente
> que noche y mar la enredan en su lazo.
>
> Y se baña en la obscura lejanía
> de su germen eterno, de su origen,
> cuando con ella Dios amanecía, . . .
> (XIV, 510)

> . . . the soul feels
> the ensnaring net of night and sea.
>
> And bathes in the dark distance
> of its eternal germ and source,
> when God awoke with it, . . .

A perennial Castilian concept of life, most successfully expressed by Jorge Manrique in the fifteenth century, is that of a river flowing into the ocean of death. It is a notion that may be related to the stoicism many observers have found in the Spanish character. Unamuno fought it bitterly, with his strident shout for immortality.[17] When confronted at last with the sea, he partially succumbed. The battle continued; faith copied the water's movement and advanced and retreated like sun-swept waves. But there is also a unique feeling of acceptance:

> Un oasis me fuiste, isla bendita;
> la civilización es un desierto
> donde la fe con la verdad se irrita;
>
> cuando llegué a tu roca llegué a puerto,
> y esperándome allí a la última cita
> sobre tu mar vi el cielo todo abierto.
> (XIV, 547)

> You were for me an oasis, blessed isle;
> civilization is a desert
> where faith is galled by truth;

17. Gerald Brenan, *The Literature of the Spanish People: From Roman Times to the Present* (New York: Meridian Books, 1957), p. 425.

> when I arrived at your rock, I arrived at port,
> and awaiting me there for my final hour,
> I saw the sky open over your sea.

At times the struggle ebbed until he seemed almost on the verge of betraying his past. Contemplating a small monument to eleven French Basques killed in the war, he realized they did not ask why: ". . . the yoke plows, / and the field is all it knows. . . . / Let us live / as ye have died, without reason: therein lies sanity . . ." (XIV, 624).

These sonnets in exile express moments of deep emotional significance—Unamuno between the sea and the sky, two blank expansions of the nothingness he feared, or two splendid extensions of the God he needed but did not know. One evening at sunset, the beauty of fading light caused hope to well up in his soul:

> Horas serenas del ocaso breve,
> cuando la mar se abraza con el cielo
> y se despierta el inmortal anhelo
> que al fundirse la lumbre, lumbre bebe.
>
> Copos perdidos de encendida nieve,
> las estrellas se posan en el suelo
> de la noche celeste, y su consuelo
> nos dan piadosas con su brillo leve.
>
> Como en concha sutil perla perdida,
> lágrimas de las olas gemebundas,
> entre el cielo y la mar sobrecogida
>
> el alma cuaja luces moribundas
> y recoge en el lecho de su vida
> el poso de sus penas más profundas.
>          (XIV, 532)

> Serene hours of brief sundown,
> when the sea and sky embrace
> and our immortal urge awakens
> and from fusing light drinks light.
>
> Lost flakes of burning snow,
> the stars perch on the soil
> of celestial night and their comfort
> compassionately offer with quiet light.

> Like a pearl lost in a subtle shell,
> or tears on the wailing waves,
> the soul overcome between sea and sky
>
> moulds the dying light
> and gathers in the lap of life
> the dregs of its deepest grief.

The immortal urge, as always, is checked by an iron hand refusing peace, and the soul confronts alone the tragic sense of life.

# The Lengthening Shadow

Unamuno wrote to preserve himself. He expected from literature the immortality that reason and time would deny to his body. At best, it was a "harsh comfort," but still his only one. While in exile at Hendaye, as his "shadow lengthened towards death" (No. 3),[18] he conceived the idea of fixing this gradual decline in words, and he began keeping a rhymed journal, published posthumously in 1953.

The journal consists of 1,755 poems written from February 26, 1928, until December 28, 1936, three days before his death. He carried little sheets of paper in his pocket, and when an idle moment presented itself or the feeling of mortality became overwhelming, he would write, dissolving himself in song. The *Cancionero* has some of his worst poetry and some of his most graceful and fluid,[19] but it is a remarkable record of the fall of a great personality. It is also a chronicle of what Unamuno saw and felt in nearly nine years, reflections on such disparate topics as the cave of Altamira and *Moby Dick*.

Typically, a writer's journal is a source of narcissistic solace and private confession. Unamuno's journal follows this pattern, of course, but in addition it emphasizes the subterranean craving for immortality, the hope of living through his reader:

18. Arabic numbers in this section refer to the order of the poems in *Cancionero*, ed. Federico de Onís (Buenos Aires: Losada, 1953).
19. Cernuda, *Poesía española contemporánea*, p. 97.

Cuando vibres todo entero
soy yo, lector, que en ti vibro.
       (March 9, 1929; No. 828)

When you tremble all over,
it is I, reader, who tremble in you.

The total impact of the *Cancionero* bluntly points up something
we are not always properly aware of: that no man puts pen to
paper for himself alone. Communication—and writing is one of
the highest forms of communication—requires two people.
Thoughts of a reader are always present in the person writing.
The acclaimed author, of course, writes directly for his public.
But the hermit in his cell glossing the Psalms, the aesthete vin-
dicating himself in the eyes of posterity, the solid keeper of a
diary—all write with someone figuratively peering over their
shoulders. The *Cancionero* recognizes this phenomenon.

It also recognizes that man's chief recourse for expression is
language—not the language of theory or of equations, but the
living, flowing, vital talk of human beings. The older Unamuno
grew, the more closely united language and poetry became:

Agavillar cada día
 ilusiones con el metro
y hacer así de éste el cetro
del reino de la ufanía.
Bailar nuestro sueño al borde
del abismo en la esperanza
de que ha de ser contradanza
con la del Señor acorde.
       (Aug. 13, 1934; No. 1665)

To bind as sheaves each day
illusion with meter,
making thus the sceptre
of our prideful kingdom.
To dance our dream on the edge
of the abyss, in hope
that it may be a counterdance
to the rhythm of the Lord.

Until the end, the seesaw of faith and despair continued. To-wards October of his final year, one notes a fragmentation of certain poems, a pathetic sense of things breaking up:

> Horas de espera, vacías;
> se van pasando los días
> sin valor,
> y va cuajando en mi pecho,
> frío, cerrado y deshecho,
> el terror.
> Se ha derretido el engaño
> ¡alimento me fue antaño!
> ¡pobre fe!
> lo que ha de serme mañana
> ...se me ha perdido la gana...
> no lo sé... !
> Cual sueño de despedida
> ver a lo lejos la vida
> que pasó,
> y entre brumas en el puerto
> espera muriendo el muerto
> que fui yo.
> (Oct. 28, 1936; No. 1743)

> Vacant, watchful hours;
> the days go by
> valueless,
> and congealing in my breast,
> exhausted, cold and closed,
> is terror.
> My illusion is consumed;
> long ago it fed me!
> poor faith!
> What will become of me tomorrow
> ...I have lost the desire...
> I do not know... !
> Like a farewell dream
> I see from afar my life
> now past;
> lost in the fogbound port,
> dying, waits the dead man
> that was I.

Two months later he wrote his last words. They prove that despite his fondness for contradictions and his abhorrence of systems, he was singularly consistent. If there is a sense of capitulation, it is belied by the very gesture of gazing at the sky:

> a qué al poner en ello tanto empeño
> aprender lo que al punto al fin se olvida
> escudriñando el implacable ceño
> —cielo desierto—del eterno dueño?
>                     (Dec. 28, 1936; No. 1755)

> why such determination
> to learn what in the end is at once forgotten,
> searching the implacable frown
> —O empty sky—of the eternal master?

Unamuno stood out sharply from the poetic fashions of his time, and today his religious poetry in particular seems to be a strange anomaly. The childlike quest for certainty, and the stubborn assertion that immortality is meaningless unless it provides for the continuity of present personality are attitudes that exhibit a painful contrast to much of the intellectually sophisticated approach to religion in the modern period. In many respects, his anguish echoes that of the ancient Hebrew prophets, and appears far removed from the quiet desperation of ordinary men. Existing like one of those crags in his sonnet, Unamuno saw the passing clouds withhold rain from him, and he remained eternally thirsty and alone.

Ortega y Gasset, in words that were to be all too prophetic, recorded the sense of loss when the rock finally fell: "Unamuno is now with death, his perennial friend and enemy. . . . He was the great Iberian in both the good and bad sense of the word. . . . For over a quarter of a century his voice sounded daily throughout Spain. Now that it has ceased forever, I fear our country will suffer a period of frightful silence."[20]

20. Quoted in Julián Marías, *Filosofía española actual*, 3rd ed. (Madrid: Espasa-Calpe, 1956), pp. 11–12.

SELECTED POETRY

OF UNAMUNO

*(In order of publication)*

*Poesías.* Bilbao: Rojas, 1907.

*Rosario de sonetos líricos.* Madrid: Impr. Española, 1911.

*El Cristo de Velázquez.* Madrid: Calpe, 1920.

*De Fuerteventura a París.* Paris: Excelsior, 1925.

*El romancero del destierro.* Buenos Aires: Edit. Alba, 1928.

*Cancionero,* ed. Federico de Onís. Buenos Aires: Losada, 1953.

*Cincuenta poesías méditas,* ed. Manuel García Blanco. Palma de Mallorca: Papeles de Son Armadans, 1958.

*Obras completas,* XIII, XIV: *Poesía,* I, II, ed. Manuel García Blanco. Madrid: Afrodisio Aguado, 1962, 1963. This competent series, the only approach to a critical edition we have of Unamuno's works, began to appear in 1950, was reprinted in 1958, and is still being added to. In the last two volumes, the reader may consult all of Unamuno's poetry except the *Cancionero* and a few scattered pieces.

ENGLISH

TRANSLATIONS

Eleanor L. Turnbull has been a devoted translator of Unamuno, but her versions ordinarily do not capture the blunt energy of the original. See *The Christ of Velázquez* (Baltimore, Md.: Johns Hopkins Press, 1951), *Poems* (Baltimore, Md.: Johns Hopkins Press, 1952), and *Ten Centuries of Spanish Poetry* (Baltimore, Md.: Johns Hopkins Press, 1955), pp. 374–405.

*The Poem Itself,* ed. Stanley Burnshaw (New York: Holt, 1960), pp. 166–71, has a literal translation with commentary on the well-known poem about a Castilian cemetery. *The Penguin Book of Spanish Verse,* ed. J. M. Cohen, revised edition (London: Penguin Books, 1960), pp. 329–32, has a prose translation of the same poem. Cohen's revisions have eliminated some of the inaccuracies of text and translation in the first edition (1956), but many still remain. And why, one wonders, in a plain prose translation, as the book is subtitled, should *corral* necessarily be "sheep-fold," or *riego* (irrigation) "gushing waters"?

Two selections from *The Christ of Velázquez,* translated by Anthony Kerrigan in *Poetry,* CI (1963), 319–21, augur well for the quality of the nine-volume translation of Unamuno's works that Mr. Kerrigan is preparing for the Bollingen Foundation. The translator is sensitive to Unamuno's forceful, biblical diction in the long meditation on the Velázquez painting, and arranges the English to correspond closely.

# II

## Antonio Machado

---

## A Few True Words

# The Outer World

In a country where very few people agree on anything, the mere mention of the name Antonio Machado spontaneously evokes the consensus that in Spanish letters he is already a classic. Such unanimous veneration is all the more remarkable because Machado's reputation is colored with political nuances. He died in exile, having fled after the fall of Barcelona in 1939, and his grave, lying just across the Pyrenees in southeastern France, inevitably became a symbol of republican Spain. A generation of writers, crushed and bewildered during the earthquake of civil war, were attracted by the probity of his modest public life, and discovered in the austerity of his style a model that most closely corresponded to their own state of mind.

While he was alive, his aloofness discouraged the usual literary coterie from developing around him. Those who knew him, including Darío, were uniformly impressed by his somber seriousness. At the age of thirty-two, he deliberately chose to isolate himself from the literary life of the capital by accepting the first of several posts he was to hold in the provincial schools of Spain. Most of his mature years were spent in the monotonous atmosphere of battered desks, chalk-stained blackboards, and routine learning. It was the perfect foil for the inner war that consumed him as he grew older. His shabby, unkempt figure, rambling alone on long walks, became a familiar sight:

> . . . yo paso, viejo y tristón.
> Dentro del pecho llevo un león.
>                              (CLV, i)[1]
>
> . . . I pass by, old and awkwardly sad.
> Within my breast, I carry a lion.

Machado's poetry is not a very promising candidate to sur-
vive the perils of translation. Devoid of striking metaphors, his
work seems flat without the background of its native music. In
Spanish, it has all the mystery and appeal of unaffected verse.
The early lyrics, with their sense of color and luminescence, are
innately Andalusian. When, at a later date, the Castilian landscape becomes his subject matter, the descriptions are more detailed, but the essence of the poetry remains the same: simplicity
and naturalness. And these are qualities that can neither be imi-
tated successfully nor transferred to another language.

Although born in Seville, from the age of eight he lived in
Madrid and was educated at the famous Institución Libre de
Enseñanza.[2] *Modernismo* disclosed to him how Spanish poetry
might be revitalized. Either through Darío, or independently, he
discovered Verlaine. Together he and Juan Ramón Jiménez
would recite the songs of autumn and empty gardens. But he
also became a devoted reader of Bécquer and Rosalía de Castro,
whose lyrics complement Verlaine. Finally, the model of Unamuno led him to reject the adornments of *modernismo* and to
refine Verlaine's influence. He ultimately responded to what
Unamuno called the "deep native note," founded upon the pressing imperative of Spanish reality and intrinsically different from
the princesses and myths of the *modernistas*.

Conflict between life and art developed into a basic theme of

1. Roman numerals refer to the arrangement of poems in *Obras* (Mexico
City: Séneca, 1940). Machado's poems are quoted by permission of Matea M.
vda. de Machado.

2. For his life, see Gabriel Pradal-Rodríguez, "Antonio Machado: Vida y
obra," *Revista Hispánica Moderna* XV (1949), 1–27. Recently, Alice McVan
has provided a more detailed account in *Antonio Machado* (New York: Hispanic Society of America, 1959). I have also consulted Manuel Tuñón de Lara,
*Antonio Machado* (Paris: Pierre Seghers, 1960). Machado himself left a bare
autobiographical sketch. See *Obras*, p. 32.

his letters and early prose. Even in 1903, as he published his first book *Solitudes* (*Soledades*) amidst the artificial music of *modernismo,* he wrote to Unamuno, ". . . the artist should love life and despise art."[3] His own life was a running battle between an overwhelming inclination towards aesthetic introspection and a guilty desire to reach a broader understanding of the surrounding world and mankind. The latter concepts he lumped together under the term "objectivity," and constantly tried to find a place for them in his poetry. Of one thing he was certain—sentiments were stronger than ideas and poems were made with emotions first and words second. Here too the influence of Unamuno was decisive.

Until he was thirty-two years old, he led the frivolous bohemian life typical of the *literatos* at the turn of the century: frequent visits to Paris, discussions in Madrid cafés, mutual and facile admiration and recrimination. Only a brooding, withdrawn nature set him off from the rest. In 1907, he decided to undergo the *oposiciones* (competitions) for a teaching post. He was successful and in May assumed his duties as a teacher of French in the ancient Castilian town of Soria, located on the banks of the river Duero. It was the beginning of a long love affair with that uncompromising, lonely region.

Naked against rocks and sky, he was forced to come to grips with himself and to begin a deeper exploration of his personality. By 1913 he could write to Unamuno, "I learned a bit in Paris, but I learned much more roaming through third-rate towns."[4] In the country he discovered a natural cycle of life and time that matched his own modesty and melancholy. Both the goodness and badness of life and people stood out boldly. The isolated dreamer of *Solitudes* received from the stark land of Castile an objective confirmation of his internal vision.

Meanwhile, the loves of bohemia merged into an adoration

3. Quoted in Geoffrey Ribbans, "Unamuno and Antonio Machado," *Bulletin of Hispanic Studies,* XXXIV (1957), 11. This study is impressive proof of Unamuno's influence upon Machado.

4. *Los complementarios,* ed. Guillermo de Torre (Buenos Aires: Losada, 1957), p. 165.

of one woman. She was sixteen. With her friends, she would stroll along one side of the Duero while Machado followed, entranced, on the other. They were married in 1909. Here, he felt, was further proof that the outside world should have claim upon his attention. Castile and his child bride Leonor seemed to signal the end of introspection, resulting in the so-called objective poetry of *Fields of Castile* (*Campos de Castilla,* 1912).

One's basic nature is never so easily rearranged, however. While the couple were in Paris, where Machado was studying under Bergson and putting the finishing touches on his second book, Leonor began to vomit blood. It was Bastille Day, 1911, and Machado's grim search through the reveling streets of Paris for a doctor took on the proportions of a nightmare. They returned almost at once to Soria. Residents still recall the untidy figure, clad in black, pushing Leonor in a wheel chair. She died August 1, 1912.

The death of the one "who planted my feet upon the earth" (CXLI) demolished the foundation of his new life, and loneliness and melancholy returned to take up permanent abode. A letter to Juan Ramón Jiménez reveals that in a moment of desperation he had contemplated suicide.[5] In reality, however, the accident of Leonor's death restored his innate disposition to its former strength. Sometime before 1907 he had written:

> Es una tarde cenicienta y mustia,
> destartalada, como el alma mía;
> y es esta vieja angustia
> que habita mi usual hipocondría.
> (LXXVII)

> It is a dull and ashen afternoon,
> shabby like my soul;
> it is this old anguish
> dwelling in my familiar hypochondria.

The grief of personal loss bestowed upon his brooding temperament a grave nobility. Of the many poems written as a result

---

5. "When I lost my wife, I considered putting a bullet through my head."—*Cartas de Antonio Machado a Juan Ramón Jiménez,* ed. Ricardo Gullón (Río Piedras: University of Puerto Rico, 1959), p. 38.

of Leonor's death, the following combines sorrow, dignity, and resignation to a remarkable degree:

> Señor, ya me arrancaste lo que yo más quería.
> Oye otra vez, Dios mío, mi corazón clamar.
> Tu voluntad se hizo, Señor, contra la mía.
> Señor, ya estamos solos mi corazón y el mar.
>
> (CXIX)

> Lord, you have torn from me what most I loved.
> Hear again, O God, my heart cry out.
> Your will, Lord, was done against mine.
> Lord, my heart and the sea are now alone.

The final line is an austere appreciation of his destiny, for the sea symbolized death, which he now faced alone.

The years immediately following the death of his wife were spent in Baeza, a time-haunted city in northern Andalusia. Shabby, desperate, and silent, he wandered through the olive groves, remembering the rocks of Soria, tormented by the suspicion that his lyric ability was declining. In those years, he began earnestly to study philosophy, going so far as to earn a degree at the University of Madrid. Although his efforts were veiled in irony (he called himself a "hackneyed philosopher"), he remarked that great poets were men who had failed as metaphysicians.

The tedious routine at Baeza and the stoically resigned cast of his mind are revealed in a long composition entitled "Poem of a Day" ("Poema de un día," CXXVIII). Machado, musing in his study, smiles wryly at himself, teacher of modern languages and former poet now relegated to a damp and seedy village. He summons up the outer world and clothes it in stately melancholy; the olive groves drenched by a thin cold rain, a peremptory clock in the corner, assorted books of philosophy, and the desultory talk of crops and weather are dignified by the quiet rhythm of his lines. In this water-logged town, the leisurely humanistic occupation of reading and writing is nothing but the "yawns of Solomon." Conversations with the townspeople are as numbing as the steady, ice-like drizzle, which itself signifies the ebbing of life into death. Despite its crushing implications,

the poem never wavers in its tone of dignified resignation, although in the closing lines we are suddenly face to face with
a spirit yearning to make one last leap for freedom:

> este yo que vive y siente
> dentro la carne mortal,
> ¡ay! por saltar impaciente
> las bardas de su corral.
>                    (CXXVIII)

> this living, feeling I
> within the mortal flesh,
> impatient to leap
> the walls of its corral!

In 1917, after his collected poetry appeared, Machado was
transferred to Segovia. In a way, it was a return to the world.
He organized a series of public lectures on science and letters.
The proximity to Madrid served to foster a collaboration with
his brother Manuel, and the two became successful playwrights.
It also allowed him to meet "Guiomar," as she is called in his
poems. Whoever she was, his response to her represents a final
effort on the part of that spirit evoked at the close of "Poem of
a Day" to soar beyond the corral of its present situation. "Nothing of what I write satisfies me, for I would like to do something that is not like anything I have done so far. You have
made me another man, and this other man has not yet sung."[6]
The lovers, who were finally separated just before the Civil War,
live again in the poems to Guiomar (CLXXIII, CLXXIV),
which record, among other things, an intense passion, the brief
flame of middle-aged love:

> . . . el nácar frío
> de tu zarcillo en mi boca,
> Guiomar, y en el calofrío
> de una amanecida loca; . . .
>                    (CLXXIV, i)

6. Concha Espina, *De Antonio Machado a su grande y secreto amor* (Madrid:
n.p., 1950), p. 23. The publication of these letters has been questioned as to
both taste and authenticity. Although lacking a scholarly format, they have an
unmistakable ring of validity.

> ... your cold pearl
> earring in my mouth,
> Guiomar, and the shiver
> of an insane dawn; ...[7]

In truth, however, love could only be another event in the
Heraclitean flow of life. Perhaps if one could remove it from the
realm of the actual, it would endure longer. Memory might be
less accurate than actuality but it could resist change. Machado
instinctively preferred such a subjective refuge. Who can gainsay
truth in the tranquillity of recollection?

> Escribiré en tu abanico:
> te quiero para olvidarte,
> para quererte te olvido.
> (CLXXIV, iii)

> I shall write on your fan:
> I love you in order to forget you,
> I forget you in order to love you.

The conflict between life and art, reality and subjectivity,
came to a head during the turbulent years of the Spanish Republic, followed by civil war. Machado celebrated the appearance of liberal democracy in 1931 by raising the tricolor over
Segovia. His education at the Institución Libre de Enseñanza had
helped make him sympathetic to the high but impractical ideals
of Azaña and his followers. In a few of his poems, certainly not
the best ones, he had consistently impugned the "inferior Spain
that prays and yawns," calling for its replacement by a Spain
"of chisel and hammer" (CXXXV). Self-deception was never
one of his traits, however, and he saw the Spanish situation with
a cold eye:

> Ya hay un español que quiere
> vivir y a vivir empieza,

---

7. I am indebted to the University of California Press, which in 1963 published translations of a number of Machado's poems in *Juan de Mairena: Epigrams, Maxims, Memoranda, and Memoirs of an Apocryphal Professor,* ed. and
trans. Ben Belitt, and which owns the English-language rights to "Otras canciones a Guiomar," for permission to include in the present volume translations
of this and the following poem.

> entre una España que muere
> y otra España que bosteza.
> Españolito que vienes
> al mundo, te guarde Dios.
> Una de las dos Españas
> ha de helarte el corazón.
>                     (CXXXVI, liii)

> There is a Spaniard who wants
> to live, and so he begins,
> between a dying Spain
> and a yawning Spain.
> Little Spaniard about
> to be born, may God keep you.
> One of the two Spains
> will freeze your heart.

Nevertheless, he came out avidly for the Spanish Republic and associated himself with its educational program. Long residence in the provinces had given him a sturdy respect for the lower classes. Henceforth, we have the strange spectacle of an introspective dreamer addressing himself to the problem of democratic culture. In the past, in order to express his philosophical ideas, he had modestly hidden behind a fictitious professor, whom he called Abel Martín. To give vent to new social points of view, he created another imaginary pedagogue, Juan de Mairena. Through this device and a few public speeches, he discussed the problem of spreading culture among the people. There was, he said, no higher rôle than to write for the people (*pueblo*). Such had been the achievement of Shakespeare and Cervantes. To those who worried that culture would be ruined by deploying it widely, he responded that to diffuse culture was to defend it. In Spain everything great was the work of the *pueblo,* not of the upper classes. The secret of the *pueblo*'s strength was to be found in the Castilian saying, "Nadie es más que nadie" ("No one is better than anyone"), meaning that however much a man may have in terms of material wealth, he can never exceed the value of being a man.[8]

8. "El poeta y el pueblo," *Obras,* pp. 472, 863–72.

In 1937 he refuted accusations of being a Marxist, stating that it was impossible for him to accept an economic interpretation of history. He did say, however, that socialism ". . . in so far as it supposes a way of living together based on equal opportunities for work and the abolition of class privileges is an unavoidable stage on the way to human justice. Clearly, it seems to me to be the great human experience of our day. . . ."[9] Machado's ideas strongly echo those of many American and European intellectuals—the liberal writers of the twenties and thirties, whose commitment to society was receiving its first sharp test on the Civil War battlefields of Spain.

Franco's rebellion created a wave of anti-intellectualism. "Ideas do not grow from fists," Machado had said as early as 1919, underlining his skepticism concerning any rebellion.[10] His own health was failing, and as the military situation worsened, the government moved him to Valencia, where he wrote the so-called "Poems of War," plus further sayings of the fictitious Juan de Mairena.

The Spain he loved collapsed in January, 1939. Crowded into an old truck with some intellectuals and wounded soldiers, he crossed the frontier into France. The limited space forced him to abandon clothing and papers, and to travel, as he had said in his subjective poetry, "ligero de equipaje" ("with little luggage"). Exhausted and ill, he found refuge in the small fishing village of Collioure, just across the border from Spain. Among its white houses, which face a sparkling bay, he dreamed his final dream on February 22. The prophetic stanza of "Self-portrait," written in 1907, came to be fulfilled:

> Y cuando llegue el día del último viaje,
> y esté al partir la nave que nunca ha de tornar,
> me encontraréis a bordo ligero de equipaje,
> casi desnudo, como los hijos de la mar.
>
> (XCVII)

9. "Discurso a las juventudes socialistas unificadas," *Obras*, p. 883. This speech was delivered May 1, 1937, during the first year of the Civil War. As early as 1918, he had written to Unamuno, "The ideas of Tolstoy [Christian socialism] will save Europe, if it is to be saved."—*Los complementarios*, p. 178.
10. *Obras*, p. 34.

When the day of the final voyage arrives,
and the ship that never returns is ready to sail,
you will find me aboard with little luggage,
nearly naked, like the children of the sea.

Speaking twenty years later, Camilo José Cela, one of the most important writers of present-day Spain, accurately expressed the still-living tragedy of Machado's death: "The most Spanish of our poets . . . cannot rest in the earth which saw him born. We Spaniards, who were not able to keep him, can only weep for him."[11]

# The Inner World

### THE BARE WORD

The reader of Machado's poetry is struck at once by the sparse style and limited vocabulary, both of which deliberately presuppose that language should restrain itself to the expression of emotions and ideas. Words may be beautiful, but they should never be joined in an opulence that outweighs content.[12] When he published *Soledades,* he wrote, ". . . the true element of poetry does not lie in the sound of words, nor in color or form, nor in a complex of sensations; but rather in a deep throbbing of the spirit; what . . . the soul . . . says in its own voice in emotional response to the world around it."[13]

To attain this goal, he borrowed one or two phrases from Bécquer and Verlaine, but mainly relied on a "few true words" (LXXXVIII) of his own.[14] The result is lean and unpretentious

11. "Hace por estas fechas veinte años," *Papeles de Son Armadans,* XII (1959), 118.
12. Ricardo Gullón, *Las secretas galerías de Antonio Machado* (Madrid: Taurus, 1958), pp. 16–17.
13. *Obras,* p. 25. His outspoken contemporary, the novelist Pío Baroja, said succinctly: "It seems to me that a person who retrieves from words not their significance but their sound is very close to being an idiot. . . ."—*The Restlessness of Shanti Andía,* trans. Anthony Kerrigan (Ann Arbor: University of Michigan Press, 1959), p. 96.
14. From Bécquer came the idea of the chimera of dreams and the ineffable

poetry. "At times I use words outside of their strict sense, but, when I do, I am aware of my error."[15] He explained that his objective was a classical style, which, for him, meant a noun plus a defining adjective. Homer, for example, called a ship hollow, more a definition than a description.[16]

"Winter Sun" illustrates the style he sought:

> Es mediodía. Un parque.
> Invierno. Blancas sendas;
> simétricos montículos
> y ramas esqueléticas.
>
> Bajo el invernadero,
> naranjos en maceta,
> y en su tonel, pintado
> de verde, la palmera.
>
> Un viejecillo dice,
> para su capa vieja:
> ";El sol, esta hermosura
> de sol!..." Los niños juegan.
>
> El agua de la fuente
> resbala, corre y sueña,
> lamiendo, casi muda,
> la verdinosa piedra.
>
> (XCVI)

---

"not-yet-seen." The use of "monotony" and "melancholy" derived from Verlaine, but it also suited his own temperament. The themes of memory and twilight were probably suggested by Verlaine's "Le souvenir avec le crépuscule. . . ." Unlike Verlaine, however, he plumbed the mystery of the twilit garden to its depth and found what his Spanish soul had already intuited: that reality was a dream. The Verlaine influence occurs during a tentative stage. Dámaso Alonso has shown how, in the second edition of *Soledades* (1907), Machado discarded the weaker sentimental poems, precisely those most indebted to Verlaine. See "Poesías olvidadas de Antonio Machado," in *Poetas españoles contemporáneos* (Madrid: Gredos, 1952), pp. 103–59. The general influence of Verlaine has been studied by Geoffrey Ribbans, "La influencia de Verlaine en Antonio Machado," *Cuadernos Hispanoamericanos*, XXXI (1957), 180–201. For the relationship to Bécquer, see Carlos Bousoño, *Teoría de la expresión poética*, 2nd ed. (Madrid: Gredos, 1956), pp. 146–53, and also José Luis Cano, *De Machado a Bousoño* (Madrid: Insula, 1955), pp. 29–39. Ricardo Gullón tends to reassert the influence of Juan Ramón Jiménez. See *Las secretas galerías*, pp. 37–40.

15. *Los complementarios*, p. 15.

16. *Obras*, p. 470. Machado once wryly remarked that his poetry was so simple that even fashionable ladies claimed to understand it (*Obras*, pp. 360–61).

It is noon. A park.
Winter. White paths;
symmetric mounds
and skeletal branches.

In the greenhouse,
orange trees in pots,
and in its green
barrel, the palm tree.

A spare old man says
into his worn cape:
"The sun, this beauty
of sun!..." The children play.

The water in the fountain
glides, runs, and dreams,
lapping almost silently
the greenish stone.

The effect of trenchant simplicity is related to the limited use of adjectives. Japanese haiku come to mind, as does Verlaine's use of single words, but the ultimate source for this kind of poetry is the Andalusian *copla* (brief folk song) and the Spanish ballad. The latter, which comprised Machado's earliest reading, is noted for its sparseness.

Only the flow of water deserves more than one descriptive word. Because water is a symbol of time, Machado always underlined its movements by a liberal use of verbs. Water and the playing children are the sole motion in a static setting. Both are indifferent to the lonely spectator shuffling along the path. Against the background of common words, the old man's exclamation acquires extra poignancy, and the reader suddenly shares the feeling of age in a way that elaborate description would not have accomplished. It is the "deep throbbing spirit ... in ... response to the world around it."

By using common words to create an uncommon effect, Machado often achieved a stark realism. "At the Burial of a Friend" piles up concrete, simple detail with an overwhelming effect:

Tierra le dieron una tarde horrible
del mes de julio, bajo el sol de fuego.

A un paso de la abierta sepultura,
había rosas de podridos pétalos,
entre geranios de áspera fragancia
y roja flor. El cielo
puro y azul. Corría
un aire fuerte y seco.

De los gruesos cordeles suspendido,
pesadamente, descender hicieron
el ataúd al fondo de la fosa
los dos sepultureros...

Y al resonar sonó con recio golpe,
solemne en el silencio.

Un golpe de ataúd en tierra es algo
perfectamente serio.

Sobre la negra caja se rompían
los pesados terrones polvorientos...

El aire se llevaba
de la honda fosa el blanquecino aliento.

—Y tú, sin sombra ya, duerme y reposa,
larga paz a tus huesos...

Definitivamente,
duerme un sueño tranquilo y verdadero.

(IV)

Earth they gave him one horrible afternoon
under the searing sun of July.

One step from the open sepulcher,
withered rose petals lay,
among pungent blooming geraniums. The sky
pure and blue. A harsh
dry air moving.

Suspended on two thick cords,
the coffin heavily descended,
guided by two gravediggers
to the bottom of the pit...

It came to rest with a thud,
harsh and solemn in the silence.

The sound of coffin striking earth
is unsurpassedly serious.

Thick dusty clods
broke upon the black box...

The breeze bore upward
a whitened breath from the deep hole.

—Now your shadow is gone, dream and rest,
long peace to your bones...

And finally
sleep a true and tranquil sleep.

Simplicity of line, limited but fundamental emotions, a sense of life lived without the interruptions of history—these are the goals Machado set for his lean vocabulary. Nowhere are they more consummately realized than in this delicate description of a fountain-filled square in which a young girl is drawing water. The fountain dreams, time flows, the wind plays with the dead leaves: all is beautiful and serene, but nothing more so than the maiden, who is perfectly beautiful and perfectly ignorant of it. In her natural act reposes the poetry of everyday living; as she breathes in the peaceful surroundings, she symbolizes the simple clarity and freshness of emotion that Machado so assiduously sought:

¡Verdes jardinillos,
claras plazoletas,
fuente verdinosa
donde el agua sueña,
donde el agua muda
resbala en la piedra!...

Las hojas de un verde
mustio, casi negras,
de la acacia, el viento
de septiembre, besa,
y se lleva algunas
amarillas, secas,
jugando, entre el polvo
blanco de la tierra.

Linda doncellita,
que el cántaro llenas
de agua transparente,

tú, al verme, no llevas
a los negros bucles
de tu cabellera,
distraídamente,
la mano morena,
ni, luego, en el limpio
cristal te contemplas...

Tú miras al aire
de la tarde bella,
mientras de agua clara
el cántaro llenas.

(XIX)

Green little gardens,
bright tiny squares,
the grey-green fountain
where the dreaming water,
the silent water,
slides over stones!...

Somber green leaves,
nearly black, on the acacia
which the September wind caresses,
carrying off the yellow withered ones,
playing with them in the white dust
on the ground.

Pretty little maiden
filling your jug
with transparent water,
when you see me, you do not touch
the dark curls
of your hair
absently
with your brown hand,
nor, later, in the clear
mirror contemplate your image...

You look at the air
of the lovely late day,
and fill your jug
with limpid water.

Thus the most overworked words in the language were revitalized. With care and persistence in poem after poem, Ma-

chado repeated his "few true words" until the cumulative effect
was one of breathtaking clarity, a "crystal legend" (VIII).

Within the restrictions of his vocabulary, symbolic meaning
plays a fundamental part. His symbols are few, but they are
vital, based upon an aching awareness of ebbing life. Among
them is the plaza, so important to the Spanish scene. All roads
lead to the plaza, especially to the plaza of the small village.
There children play, old men dream, and women dressed in
black walk to Mass. There, also, the inevitable fountain flows
symbolically. The plaza offers a world of memory and illusion,
where only grief is steadfast and clear:

> La fuente de la piedra
> vertía su eterno
> cristal de leyenda.
>
> Cantaban los niños,
> canciones ingenuas,
> de un algo que pasa
> y que nunca llega:
> la historia confusa
> y clara la pena.
>                              (VIII)
>
> The stone fountain
> spilled its eternal
> crystal legend.
>
> The children were singing
> artless songs
> of something that passes
> and never arrives:
> the story confused,
> the grief clear.

The voices of singing children stand for purity of emotion and
lost youth. They hover in the background of many of his poems,
their sweet sounds emphasizing the remorseless process of aging,
their lingering tone one of memory's chords.

The plaza, however, is not always filled with childish voices
and bubbling fountains. It is often a "dead plaza" (X), where

the afternoon foreshadows an ultimate silence, Cupid dreams
without love, and life, symbolized by water, is cold and still:

> Las ascuas de un crepúsculo morado
> detrás del negro cipresal humean...
> En la glorieta en sombra está la fuente
> con su alado y desnudo Amor de piedra,
> que sueña mudo. En la marmórea taza
> reposa el agua muerta.
>
> (XXXII)

> The embers of purple dusk
> smolder behind the dark cypress grove...
> In the shadowed arbor stands the fountain
> with its naked winged Cupid of stone,
> mutely dreaming. In the cold marble cup
> the dead water rests.

Machado was an inveterate walker, and *el camino* (the road)
is another of his favorite symbols. "A labyrinth of streets / leads
into the deserted plaza" (X). Along dusty roads in the late
afternoon he would dream his way, bemused by the morbid
echoes of sun and filled with a poignant sense of something
lost. Roads become synonymous with time, and man's reality
was defined by his movement on them:

> Caminante, son tus huellas
> el camino, y nada más;
> caminante, no hay camino,
> se hace camino al andar.
> Al andar se hace camino
> y al volver la vista atrás
> se ve la senda que nunca
> se ha de volver a pisar.
> Caminante, no hay camino,
> sino estelas en la mar.
>
> (CXXXVI, xxix)

> Traveler, your footprints
> are the road, and nothing more;
> traveler, there is no road,
> your walking makes it so.

Walking makes the road,
and on looking back,
one sees the path
that will never be trod again.
Traveler, there is no road,
only the ocean's wake.

### THE VISION OF DREAMS

". . . nearly always it seems to me
I dream everything I see. . . ."
        Santa Teresa, *Libro de su vida*
        (New York: Doubleday, 1961), p. 284

Among the "few true words" of Machado's vocabulary, two
of the most cherished are the verb *soñar* (to dream) and its
substantive *sueño*. They possess a special radius of meaning in
his work, and more than the other tools of his lexicon, enable
us to understand the way he looked at reality.

The venerable *sueño* tradition of Hispanic letters—the sense
that life is an illusion—pervaded many of the chief works of
the classical period. In Calderón's seventeenth-century drama
*Life Is a Dream* (*La vida es sueño*), Segismundo concludes in
a beautifully alliterative line: "y los sueños sueños son" ("and
dreams themselves are dreams"), forcing the reader, as in the
case of Cervantes, to draw his own conclusions about the levels
of illusion that envelop life. The philosopher Santayana, revealing his Spanish heritage, said: "Relapses into dreams are to
be expected in a being whose brief existence is so like a dream.
. . ."[17] But the direct link to Machado in this tradition is Bécquer's *Rimas* of 1870. Bécquer's mind was teeming with such a
vast population of dreams—weird and fabulous children of his
imagination—that he had difficulty distinguishing between
things that he had imagined and things that had actually hap-
pened to him. From the writers of the Golden Age, for whom

17. *Interpretation of Poetry and Religion* (New York: Harper, 1957), p. 1.
For the rôle of dreams in Machado, see Ramón de Zubiría, *La poesía de Antonio Machado* (Madrid: Gredos, 1955), *passim*, and José Luis Cano, *De Machado a Bousoño*, pp. 13–28.

dreams were a metaphor for the illusory nature of life, the *sueño* theme develops in Bécquer's time into a mysterious involvement with the process of literary creation, and it is exactly at this point that Machado picks up the tradition and brings it into the twentieth century.

The manifold meanings of *soñar* and *sueño* in Machado's work cannot be compressed into a ready formula, for they are deeply rooted in his character and are as complex to define as character itself. The introspective, melancholy man spent many hours wending his way upon lonely paths, and as his senses peacefully opened to the landscape through which he wandered, he could justifiably begin one of his most famous poems: "I slowly dream the roads / of afternoon" (XI). "This dream insomnia of mine," he called it in a later composition (CXXVII).

These are not the daydreams of ordinary mortals, whose senses dilate and who live momentarily at deeper levels of feeling before resuming their mild routine. For Machado, *soñar*—to dream while awake—was a continual state of mind, a means of perception. In a simile reminiscent of Santa Teresa, he likened the mind to a gallery, a series of long winding corridors which remain empty until the winds of memory, blending past and present, fill them with echoes that reverberate in the form of poetry. Then the mind becomes a road of dreams:

> Tú sabes las secretas galerías
> del alma, los caminos de los sueños,
> y la tarde tranquila
> donde van a morir...
>
>     (LXX)

> You know the secret galleries
> of the soul, the roads of dreams,
> and the tranquil afternoon
> where they will die...

Like A. E. Housman's ". . . happy highways where I went / And cannot come again," Machado's road of dreams traces its way from the past through the present to disappear once more into dusk. But Machado insisted upon traveling again those happy highways. *Soñar* unites memory and the actual moment, and expands consciousness by giving it an underlying emotional continuity. When the poet made the fountain ask, "Does my present song / remind you of a distant dream?" (VI), he equated the reality of here and now with the recollection of the past, stating the purpose of his poetry: to sing that which is lost, and, in a sense, to recover it, bathed in a deeper light. His obvious predilection for the evening hour befits that time of penumbra between night and day when visions most easily come and go, and experience is tinged with nostalgia.

Machado poignantly realized that his dreams were as insubstantial as air, subject to the gusts of change brought about by time. In the following poem, the shimmering *sueño* of sun and rain suddenly vanishes:

> Desgarrada la nube; el arco iris
> brillando ya en el cielo,
> y en un fanal de lluvia
> y sol el campo envuelto.
>
> Desperté. ¿Quién enturbia
> los mágicos cristales de mi sueño?
> Mi corazón latía
> atónito y disperso.
>
> ...¡El limonar florido,
> el cipresal del huerto,
> el prado verde, el sol, el agua, el iris...
> ¡el agua en tus cabellos!...
>
> Y todo en la memoria se perdía
> como una pompa de jabón al viento.
> (LXII)

> The tattered cloud; the rainbow
> shining now in the sky,
> and in a shimmering tower of rain
> and sun the field enfolded.
>
> I awoke. Who darkened
> the magic windows of my dreams?
> My heart was beating
> aghast and confused.

...The blooming lemon grove,
the garden's cypress stand,
the green meadow, the sun, the water, the rainbow...
the water in your hair!...

    All into my memory disappeared
like a soap bubble in the wind.

A large segment of the poetry of *Soledades* is concerned with the recovery of dreams that have disappeared into memory. The poet delves into the storehouse of the mind and touches the waiting chords which respond with the basic vocabulary of emotional life:

    Tal vez la mano, en sueños,
del sembrador de estrellas,
hizo sonar la música olvidada

    como una nota de la lira inmensa,
y la ola humilde a nuestros labios vino
de unas pocas palabras verdaderas.
        (LXXXVIII)

    In dreams perhaps the hand
of the sower of stars
made the forgotten music sound

    like the note of an immense lyre,
and the humble wave to our lips came,
bearing a few true words.

By perceiving through the magic eye of dreams the subjective continuity of life, one can also enrich self-understanding:

    Y podrás conocerte, recordando
del pasado soñar los turbios lienzos,
en este día triste en que caminas
con los ojos abiertos.
        (LXXXIX)

    And you may know yourself by remembering
the murky canvases of past dreams
on this sad day while you walk
with open eyes.

The overwhelming impression of *Soledades* is that all of life is a melancholy dream with poignant moments of beauty woven together by poetry in the lengthening shadows of afternoon. But Machado, while basically a subjective poet intent upon painting landscapes of the mind as Verlaine had done, occasionally projected himself beyond his lonely vision, and in a very fine late poem extended his concept of *soñar*. *Soñar* is the way in which we all see, and *sueño* is ultimately a matter of subjective perception. Ortega y Gasset remarked that each life is a point of view upon the universe. In the following poem, Machado reveals the different points of view (disparate, lonely dreams) of four passengers on a train winding its way through the Guadarrama mountains to Madrid:

Iris de la noche
A D. Ramón del Valle-Inclán

Hacia Madrid, una noche,
va el tren por el Guadarrama.
En el cielo, el arco iris
que hacen la luna y el agua.
¡Oh luna de abril, serena,
que empuja las nubes blancas!

La madre lleva a su niño,
dormido, sobre la falda.
Duerme el niño, y todavía
ve el campo verde que pasa,
y arbolillos soleados,
y mariposas doradas.

La madre, ceño sombrío
entre un ayer y un mañana,
ve unas ascuas mortecinas
y una hornilla con arañas.

Hay un trágico viajero,
que debe ver cosas raras,
y habla solo y, cuando mira,
nos borra con la mirada.

Yo pienso en campos de nieve
y en pinos de otras montañas.

Y tú, Señor, por quien todos
vemos y que ves las almas,
dinos si todos, un día
hemos de verte la cara.

(CLVIII, x)

Night Rainbow
For D. Ramón del Valle-Inclán

Toward Madrid, one night,
the train goes through the Guadarrama.
In the sky, the rainbow
made by moon and mist.
O April moon, serene,
pressing against white clouds!

The mother holds her child
asleep upon her lap.
The child sleeps and still
he sees the passing green land,
the sun-drenched little trees,
and golden butterflies.

The mother darkly frowning
between yesterday and tomorrow
sees some dying embers
and a kitchen stove on spider legs.

There is a tragic traveler
who must see strange things,
who speaks alone, and when he looks,
erases us with his glance.

I think of fields of snow
and pines of other mountains.

And you, Lord, by whom
we all see and who sees our souls,
tell us if we all, one day,
shall see your face.

Each traveler is locked in his subjective world, one which
Machado apprehends but does not analyze. The child is actually
asleep, yet his dream is no less a waking vision—in Machado's
sense—than the practical bleak memories of the mother. As
for the poet, surrounded by these monads, self-contained entities

of subjective thought, he thinks of his own sorrow symbolized by the pines of Soria where his wife lies buried. In the final stanza, over and above the ordinary religious question, the poet is asking: Can any of us see beyond ourselves to others, to reality, to God, to a unifying vision? On the whole, Machado thought not, although tentatively he reconsiders the problem in some of his epigrammatic verse. He was gravely resigned to the inescapable subjectivity of our perception. Each of us dreams our own road, along which we wander into the dying light of afternoon.

# Strong Ungrateful Land

The reality of Castile is uncompromising. After the soft pleasant countryside of France, the traveler climbs the Pyrenees and enters upon a grim plateau. An ocean of tumbling granite is dotted here and there with poplar trees and green oases, and presided over by a sky of incredible blue. In winter a sharp cold wind penetrates the body. Shepherds wrapped in cloaks huddle and brood over their flocks. Little towns of cobbled streets and time-worn houses are filled with people whose faces, like the land which nourishes them, are stern, strong, and reticent. This is Castile, the region which bled itself white for the preservation of religious unity in Europe, the nucleus of the Spanish nation, whose language is now spoken by one hundred and forty million people. Machado's temperament responded to its stark beauty. If reality must intrude, let it be this somber landscape of rocks and scarlet hills, peopled by dogged peasants, who live as if the anecdotes of history did not exist.

The prologue to *Fields of Castile* is a revealing and, at the same time, contradictory document. He had begun to suspect the possible sterility of his vision and phrased his doubt in terms of a paradox: "A man attentive to himself . . . smothers the only authentic voice he can hear—his own. . . ."[18] Nevertheless, the objects of reality could also seem to be an illusion, for man

18. *Obras*, pp. 27–28.

was the victim of a double mirage. Returning to his first book, he postulated the only solution: to dream his dream. But now the objective elements were to assume a new importance. The world of Castile became integrated into his vision, reinforcing it. That is the extent of his so-called objectivity, merely another synthesis of himself and the world. The twilit plaza was replaced by the rocks of Castile, the autumn garden by the dry *meseta*. And although metaphors increased in number and in boldness, the technique remained basically the same.[19]

"On the Banks of the Duero" blends the subjective present and the historical past. On a burning July afternoon, the poet slowly climbs rocky ground, treading occasionally upon pungent mountain herbs. Below him, scarlet hills are scattered about like the remains of a war harness. The river Duero traces the curve of a crossbow on its way through the oaken heart of Castile, leading the poet to a comparison of past and present:

> Castilla miserable, ayer dominadora,
> envuelta en sus andrajos desprecia cuanto ignora.
> ¿Espera, duerme o sueña? ¿La sangre derramada
> recuerda, cuando tuvo la fiebre de la espada?
> Todo se mueve, fluye, discurre, corre o gira;
> cambian la mar y el monte y el ojo que los mira.
> ¿Pasó? Sobre sus campos aún el fantasma yerra
> de un pueblo que ponía a Dios sobre la guerra.
>
> La madre en otro tiempo fecunda en capitanes
> madrastra es hoy apenas de humildes ganapanes.
> Castilla no es aquella tan generosa un día,
> cuando Myo Cid Rodrigo el de Vivar volvía,
> ufano de su nueva fortuna, y su opulencia,
> a regalar a Alfonso los huertos de Valencia; . . .
>
> (XCVIII)

19. Azorín quickly grasped this, noting that ". . . landscape and feeling . . . are identical; the poet transfers himself to the object described and through his means of describing it, reveals his own spirit."—*Clásicos y modernos,* 3rd ed. (Buenos Aires: Losada, 1949), p. 78. Despite a considerable increase in vocabulary, the basic technique of the "identifying" adjective is still the same. Ortega y Gasset, commenting on the use of *cárdeno* (livid) and *pardo* (brown), pointed out that they constituted a minimum adornment. *Mocedades,* 2nd ed. (Buenos Aires: Espasa-Calpe, 1943), p. 146.

Miserable Castile, dominant yesterday,
now wrapped in rags, despising all she does not know.
Does she wait, sleep, dream, or remember
the blood that flowed with the fever of her sword?
Everything moves, flows, glides, runs, revolves,
the seas and mountains change and the eye that watches them.
Is it past? Over her land still wanders the ghost
of men who gave to God command of war.

Fertile mother, in other times, of captains
is today barely stepmother to humble drudges.
Castile is not the generous one of yore
when My Cid Rodrigo of Vivar returned,
boastful of new fortune and opulence,
to offer the gardens of Valencia to Alfonso; . . .

The historical past of anecdote is made part of the essential past, which is the emotion of events recreated through dreams. In reality, there is no past. Everything is in a state of Heraclitean flux: "moves, flows, glides, runs, revolves."

The people who inhabit the Castilian plain appealed to Machado because of their bare honesty, his own goal in poetry. But he did not idealize them. He remarked their astuteness, suspicious eyes, and high cheekbones (XCIX). They were not romantic *hidalgos* but laborers, tinged with the curse of Cain, serving a sanguine and fierce Old Testament deity. In the historical backwater of these people lay the true character of Spain, and not in the gypsy-ridden south. Machado sensed that Castilian austerity brought the lonesome problem of living and dying to the surface, leaving man face to face with whatever he could make of the human dilemma:

¡Oh tierra ingrata y fuerte, tierra mía!
¡Castilla, tus decrépitas ciudades!
¡La agria melancolía
que puebla tus sombrías soledades!

¡Castilla varonil, adusta tierra,
Castilla del desdén contra la suerte,
Castilla del dolor y de la guerra,
tierra inmortal, Castilla de la muerte!

(CII)

> O strong ungrateful land, my land!
> Castile, your decrepit cities!
> The bitter melancholy
> that peoples your dark loneliness!
>
> Virile Castile, stern land,
> Castile disdaining fortune,
> Castile of grief and war,
> immortal land, Castile of death!

Epithets of decay and ruin, indicative of the underlying melancholy of *Soledades,* suddenly multiply as Machado's sadness found its natural abode. The dreamer in the plaza seeks out ruins. In a Castilian town at night, the destruction wrought by time is all around:

> ¡Soria fría, *Soria pura,*
> *cabeza de Extremadura,*[20]
> con su castillo guerrero
> arruinado, sobre el Duero;
> con sus murallas roídas
> y sus casas denegridas!
>
> ¡Muerta ciudad de señores,
> soldados o cazadores;
> de portales con escudos
> de cien linajes hidalgos,
> y de famélicos galgos,
> de galgos flacos y agudos,
> que pululan
> por las sórdidas callejas,
> y a la medianoche ululan,
> cuando graznan las cornejas!
>
> ¡Soria fría! La campana
> de la audiencia da la una.
> Soria, ciudad castellana
> ¡tan bella! bajo la luna.
>                    (CXIII, vi)

20. The italicized words are taken from the city's coat-of-arms. Since it had been purged of Arabs, Soria was pure. In those days, Soria, in northern Castile, was the leading city of the area bordering on Arab territory. As the Christians gradually pushed back the Arabs, Extremadura, the name given to such territory, moved to its present southwestern location.

Cold Soria, *pure Soria,*
*leader of Extremadura,*
with its warrior castle
ruined on the Duero;
with its gnawed walls
and blackened houses!

Dead city of *señores,*
soldiers or hunters;
of portals with coats of arms
of a hundred noble lines,
and of ravenous greyhounds,
lean, sharp greyhounds,
swarming
in the sordid streets
and howling at midnight
when the night owls croak!

Cold Soria! The courthouse
bell strikes one.
Soria, Castilian city,
—so beautiful!—under the moon.

The lesson of time and change imparted by these beautiful but ruined Castilian cities coincided with the death of his wife. Shortly thereafter, he was beset by a growing sense of decline in his talent. The subjective dreamer of *Solitudes* had tasted of something outside himself. With its disappearance, it seemed likely that the magic of memory and dreams would also fail:

. . . mas falta el hilo que el recuerdo anuda
al corazón, el ancla en su ribera,
o estas memorias no son alma. Tienen,
en sus abigarradas vestimentas,
señal de ser despojos del recuerdo,
la carga bruta que el recuerdo lleva.
Un día tornarán, con luz del fondo ungidos,
los cuerpos virginales a la orilla vieja.

                                      (CXXV)

. . . but missing is the thread that memory ties
to the heart, the anchor on the bank;
these memories are not of the soul. They have,
in their motley garments,

the semblance of memory's remains,
the crude cargo that memory keeps.
One day, anointed with deeper light,
the pure bodies will return to their old shore.

From now on, he was a philosopher-poet as he waited patiently for the hope of these last two lines to be fulfilled.

# Of Time, Death, and God

As Machado listened in 1910 to the lectures of Henri Bergson at the Collège de France, he must have been profoundly affected. Bergson's theory of intuition seemed, however vaguely, to reflect a great deal that was present in Machado's poetical use of memory and dreams. The professorial idol of the Collège de France had long insisted that intelligence, while perfectly capable of conceiving of reality in geometric rational terms, could only distort vital experience, which must be understood through intuition. Intelligence can measure reality and divide it into separate elements, but only intuition can break through the limitations of intellect and identify itself with a deeper and more vital reality. For intuition, Machado must have been tempted to substitute the word poetry, as he comprehended it. His musings in twilit plazas and barren Castilian fields had proven to him the limitations of intelligence. He was not content with merely cataloguing the fountains, the old men, and the ruined buildings; instead, he was attracted to their deeper reality, which he could discover through memory and dreams, his form of the intuition that Bergson was now sophisticatedly proposing as an enhanced view of reality.

But it was Bergson's theory of time that really awakened the interest of the Spanish poet attending the crowded lectures in Paris. The chief knowledge uncovered by intuition is that man is a creature of time, not the time that the intellect compartmentalizes into seconds and minutes, but something that Bergson called "duration." The lectures Machado heard in 1910 were probably the basis of Bergson's celebrated book *Creative*

*Evolution,* published one year later, in which the following passage appears: "Duration is the continuous progression of the
past which gnaws into the future, and swells as it advances. . . .
[Man's] past is prolonged in its totality in his present, and remains there actual and active."[21] This sense of the past in the
present haunts nearly every page of *Soledades;* poem after
poem swells with the presence of a candid, lost illusion:

> ¡Y algo nuestro de ayer, que todavía
> vemos vagar por estas calles viejas!
>
> (III)
>
> And something that yesterday was ours, and still
> we see wandering these ancient streets!

The word *algo* is purposefully vague, for, as Machado said
in another poem, the details of the past may be confused, but
the grief—that is, the emotion—is always crystal clear. The
continuous progression of the past into the present is controlled
by memory, which, according to Bergson, is what consciousness
consists of when reduced to its essential characteristic. In
Machado's words, the corridors of the mind are empty until
filled by the winds of memory.

After receiving such an impressive corroboration of his youthful ideas, Machado outlined, in 1931, a concept of poetry that
is quite frankly Bergsonian. The poet, said Machado, following
closely Bergson's theory of time as duration, is the individual
most fitted to explore the vital flow of time. Reason and logic
account for ideological verse and do not stress the flow of time;
in fact, as Bergson had explained, the intelligence, being capable only of dividing reality into blocks, is unable to grasp the
basic nature of the stream of time and change that shapes reality, is unwilling to let itself go—in Bergson's phrase, to jump
into the water to see if it can swim. Intuition, which in Bergson's philosophy becomes a means of knowledge, is for Machado the inspirational fount of poetry, the *sueño* of his early

21. Quoted in Leonard Cabell Pronko, *The World of Jean Anouilh* (Berkeley:
University of California Press, 1961), p. 216, n. 21.

days now clothed in garments cut in the style of the Collège de France. As for the intellect, it had never sung, insisted Machado, nor was its mission to sing. Henceforth, poetry was to be the "essential [intuited] word in time."[22]

Machado went a step beyond his master, for he saw that to define man philosophically as a creature of time gave terrible confirmation to human finitude. He was too much of a Spaniard to overlook this conclusion, and he emphasized that the themes of poetry written in the stream of time would be unrest, anguish, fear, resignation, hope, and impatience. Gradually he came to accent anguish above other themes, unwittingly aligning himself with European existentialism. But for the moment, he began to reflect an obsessive preoccupation with time. "To live is to devour time: to hope. And no matter how transcendental our hope, it will always be the hope of continuing to hope." "Would the poet sing," asks Juan de Mairena rhetorically, "without the anguish of time?"[23] Hell he envisioned as a place where Satan sits winding a huge clock.

Driven by these notions, Machado wrote numerous aphoristic poems, called "Proverbs and Songs" (CXXXVI, CLXI). One of the most famous is the deceptively simple, "Hoy es siempre todavía" (CLXI, viii). Rendered almost impossible to translate by the flatness of the English "still" (*todavía*), it means that today, the present moment, is the extent of time. The line consists entirely of verbs and adverbs, a triumph for Machado's chief device of expressing time by means of verbs. The sound of clocks, the flow of water, and the theme of travel have all been noted as implanting a sense of time.[24] To these

---

22. *Poesía española*, ed. Gerardo Diego (Madrid: Signo, 1932), pp. 76–78. Machado echoes closely the reservations of A. E. Housman concerning the intellect: "The intellect is not the fount of poetry . . . it may actually hinder its production, and . . . it cannot be trusted to recognize poetry when produced. . . ."—*The Name and Nature of Poetry* (New York: Macmillan, 1944), p. 37.

23. *Obras*, pp. 478–79.

24. Richard Predmore, "El tiempo en la poesía de Antonio Machado," *PMLA*, LXIII (1948), 696–701. Luis Rosales has quite rightly remarked that *todavía* is the axis upon which all of Machado's poetry turns. See "Muerte y resurrección

should be added the numerous metaphors of spinning. *Golpe*
is the ticking of a clock and the sound of earth striking a coffin:

> Daba el reloj las doce... y eran doce
> golpes de azada en tierra...
> ...¡Mi hora!—grité—... El silencio
> me respondió:—No temas;
> tú no verás caer la última gota
> que en la clepsidra tiembla.
>
> Dormirás muchas horas todavía
> sobre la orilla vieja,
> y encontrarás una mañana pura
> amarrada tu barca a otra ribera.
>
> (XXI)

> The clock struck twelve... twelve
> thuds of the spade on earth...
> ..."My hour!" I cried... Silence
> answered: "Do not fear;
> you will never see the last drop
> tremble in the water clock.
>
> "You will sleep yet many hours
> on the old shore,
> and one fresh morning find
> your bark fastened to another bank."

The correlative of time is death. "Man would not have invented the clock if he did not believe in death," said Juan de
Mairena.[25] In one of the poems written early in his career, there
was already a brilliant condensation of the time-death motif:

> Al borde del sendero un día nos sentamos.
> Ya nuestra vida es tiempo, y nuestra sola cuita
> son las desesperantes posturas que tomamos
> para aguardar... Mas Ella no faltará a la cita.
>
> (XXXV)

> One day we sit down at the side of the road.
> Our life is now time, and our only care

de Antonio Machado," *Cuadernos Hispanoamericanos* Nos. 11–12 (Sept.–Dec.
1949), p. 477.
  25. *Obras*, p. 666.

the maddening postures we assume
while waiting... But She will not fail to meet us.

If we understand the sea as symbolizing death—"Our lives
are rivers emptying into the sea which is death," read the celebrated lines from Jorge Manrique, Machado's favorite poet—
then several of his aphoristic poems become clearer:

> Todo hombre tiene dos
> batallas que pelear:
> en sueños lucha con Dios;
> y despierto, con el mar.
> (CXXXVI, xxviii)

> Every man has two
> battles to wage:
> in dreams he fights with God;
> awake, with the sea.

> Morir... ¿Caer como gota
> de mar en el mar inmenso?
> ¿O ser lo que nunca he sido:
> uno, sin sombra y sin sueño,
> un solitario que avanza
> sin camino y sin espejo?
> (CXXXVI, xlv)

> To die... To fall like a drop
> of the sea into the immense sea?
> Or to be what I have never been:
> one, without shadow or dream,
> a solitary figure advancing
> without road or mirror?

The possibilities for that spiritual state seemed very slim,
whence his feeling of anguish, becoming at times, as in Unamuno, a struggle with God. The great Basque had said in *The
Tragic Sense of Life* (1913) that man created God because he
needed him to quench his thirst for immortality. Machado often
referred to the god "who is made" (CXLIII), and in "Profes-
sion of Faith" presented his own concept of the Trinity, one
not found in any standard catechism:

El Dios que todos llevamos,
el Dios que todos hacemos,
el Dios que todos buscamos
y que nunca encontraremos.
Tres dioses o tres personas
del solo Dios verdadero.
(CXXXVII, vi)

The God we all carry,
the God we all make,
the God we all seek
and never shall find.
Three gods or three persons
of the one true God.

To call him an atheist is too easy. He was a sorrowful skeptic,
a man who felt the need of God but could not find him. Even
when God invaded his dreams, it could only be as the greatest
illusion of all, for Machado never tried to prove anything by
his visions:

Ayer soñé que veía
a Dios y que a Dios hablaba;
y soñé que Dios me oía...
Después soñé que soñaba.
(CXXXVI, xxi)

Yesterday I dreamed that I saw
God and talked to him;
and I dreamed that God heard me...
Then I dreamed that I was dreaming.

# One Day the Mute Will Speak

Although a poet is often a philosopher *manqué,* as Machado
once observed, not every poet can write philosophical
verse, and frequently the muse and philosophy make unhappy
bedfellows. Machado sensed this, and he restricted his philosophical poetry to a string of ironical, ambiguous, sometimes
effective maxims. As for writing philosophy itself, he was even
more diffident and hid behind two imaginary professors, whose

fragmentary observations he pretended to be collecting, as long ago Cervantes had employed the ruse of the Arabic chronicler of Don Quixote. Critics are not unanimous, but, on the whole, it seems evident that the contact with philosophy was unfortunate for Machado's grave lyric voice, or perhaps merely coincided with the natural decline of the talent that had produced *Soledades* and *Campos de Castilla.* Although he intermittently wrote great poetry until his death, his late verse does not sustain the same level of excellence exhibited by the poetry written between 1901, the date of his first published poem, and 1917.[26]

As for the utterances of Abel Martín and Juan de Mairena, they are simultaneously frustrating and rewarding, and present problems that lie beyond the scope of this book. Two chief themes—*la nada* (nothingness) and *lo otro* (otherness)—reflect the principal preoccupations of European existentialism, of which Machado was probably ignorant at the time. Leafing through a translation of Heidegger in 1933, he ironically remarked that, had he known Heidegger before, he would have taken with greater seriousness the metaphysical phantasies of Abel Martín, the first of his apocryphal professors.[27]

The artfulness and tentative cast of his aphoristic rhymes conceal an ironic, honest man, committed to no elaborate philosophy and refusing the refuge of dogma. The retiring rural schoolmaster, whose wars were all inward, eschewed in old age the pose of a savant:

> Doy consejo, a fuer de viejo;
> nunca sigas mi consejo.
>
> (CLXI, xciv)

26. Dámaso Alonso, the dean of Spanish literary critics, judges Machado's philosophical poetry to be lacking in the principal requirement for authentic verse set forth by the poet himself—the intuitive rendering of immediate experience against the background of flowing time. Instead, the gnomic poetry limits itself to an exercise in definition in which the sense of temporality is suppressed. See "Fanales de Antonio Machado," in *Cuatro poetas españoles* (Madrid: Gredos, 1962), pp. 137–85.

27. Antonio Sánchez Barbudo, "El pensamiento de 'Abel Martín' y 'Juan de Mairena' y su relación con la poesía de Antonio Machado," *Hispanic Review,* XXIII (1954), 145. This is the most thoroughly informed study of the relationship between Machado's philosophy and his poetry.

> I give advice by right of age;
> never follow my advice.

He remained free to contradict himself, proving to be nearly as nimble as Unamuno in this exercise. But most of all, he was free to be honest. The man who could write, as his years drifted downhill, a three-line negation of his inward bent, and, in fact, an apparent denial of *sueños* and memories, is one to command respect:

> En mi soledad
> he visto cosas muy claras,
> que no son verdad.
> (CLXI, xvii)

> In my solitude
> I have seen very clear things,
> which are not true.

More than a denial, it is a qualification, for he was not completely invalidating the position of the introspective dreamer of *Soledades*. At this stage in his life, he had been deeply influenced by the problem of communication posed in his reading of philosophy. Thus, he wrote in the same vein:

> Poned atención:
> un corazón solitario
> no es un corazón.
> (CLXI, lxvi)

> Mark it well:
> a solitary heart
> is not a heart.

But if we take him too literally, we are reprimanded by this trenchant aphorism, which deposits everything once again into the lap of phantasy:

> Se miente más de la cuenta
> por falta de fantasía:
> también la verdad se inventa.
> (CLXI, xlvi)

One often lies
through lack of phantasy:
truth is also invented.

Weaving in and out of the labyrinth of these playful proverbs, finding in them a fragmentary summary of his views on
life and poetry, we renew our admiration for this simple yet
profound man. Despite the diffidence and ruling melancholy
of his character, the final note is never despairing. He hoped
that one day we might all see and speak from the depths of
our hearts, and know the deeper levels of life that he had
modestly labored to reveal:

Tu profecía, poeta.
—Mañana hablarán los mudos:
el corazón y la piedra.
        (CLXI, xcviii)

Your prophecy, poet.
—Tomorrow the mute will speak:
the heart and the stone.

SELECTED WORKS OF
MACHADO
(*In order of publication*)

*Soledades.* Madrid: Impr. de A. Alvarez, 1903.
*Soledades, galerías y otros poemas.* Madrid: Pueyo, 1907.
*Campos de Castilla.* Madrid: Renacimiento, 1912.
*Nuevas canciones.* Madrid: Mundo Latino, 1924.
*Juan de Mairena. Sentencias, donaires, apuntes y recuerdos de un pro-
fesor apócrifo.* Madrid: Espasa-Calpe, 1936.

For Machado's collected works, consult *Obras* (Mexico City: Séneca,
1940). This edition, prepared by José Bergamín, contains nearly all
writings published during his lifetime. The so-called *Obras completas*
(Madrid: Plenitud, 1957) lacks "Poesías de la guerra," as well as several articles and speeches. Diverse notes, including letters to Unamuno,
were published by Guillermo de Torre in *Los complementarios* (Buenos
Aires: Losada, 1957).

ENGLISH
TRANSLATIONS

Recently there have been several English translations. Willis Barnstone, *Eighty Poems of Antonio Machado* (New York: Las Américas,

1959) is outstanding. Barnstone, a poet himself, has captured Machado's tone remarkably well. The translations in Alice Jane McVan's *Antonio Machado* (New York: Hispanic Society of America, 1959) were done by several hands and are disappointing. They violate Machado's own tenets of style and make him seem verbose. The same may be said for most of the efforts in Eleanor L. Turnbull, *Ten Centuries of Spanish Poetry* (Baltimore, Md.: Johns Hopkins Press, 1955), pp. 406–25. *Thirty Spanish Poems of Love and Exile,* translated by Kenneth Rexroth (San Francisco: The City Lights Bookshop, 1956) includes poems by Machado, translated freely but well. In the interesting volume edited by Stanley Burnshaw, *The Poem Itself* (New York: Holt, 1960), pp. 172-81, Paul Rogers has provided some literal translations with helpful commentary. J. B. Trend's *Antonio Machado* (Oxford: Dolphin, 1953) includes numerous translations which attempt to re-create the original Spanish rhythm with disturbing results. Also taking freedom, but with more success, is John Frederick Nims, who translated three poems for *Poetry,* XCVIII (1961), 384–85.

*The Sixties,* No. 4 (1960), pp. 4–15, offers examples of Machado translated by various hands, including Barnstone. Robert Bly's effort is very good indeed. *The Penguin Book of Spanish Verse,* ed. J. M. Cohen (London: Penguin Books, 1960), pp. 344–51, provides prose translations for eleven poems. Several translators have contributed a representative selection of Machado's work to *An Anthology of Spanish Poetry from Garcilaso to García Lorca,* ed. Angel Flores (New York: Anchor, 1961), pp. 231–69. The renditions are all well done, but Kate Flores comes closest to Machado's lean, spare, occasionally delicate tone.

Worthy to be included among the best English translations of Antonio Machado are those by Charles Tomlinson in *The Hudson Review,* XV (1962), 197–211. The rendition of "Poema de un día: Meditaciones rurales" (*Obras,* CXXVIII) is particularly fortunate. Essential to the Machado canon because of its majestic melancholy and stubborn hope, the poem had heretofore defied successful translation. To express Machado's irregularly rhymed *octosílabos,* Tomlinson chose a short line composed of either one or two beats, with an occasional rhyme. The effect is very close to the original:

> Invierno. Cerca del fuego.
> Fuera llueve un agua fina,
> que ora se trueca en neblina,
> ora se torna aguanieve.
>
> Winter:
>     the fireside:

> in the street
> a fine rain falls
> alternately as mist or sleet.

In a conversation with the author, Tomlinson remarked that he thought the short indented lines gave the effect of a person thinking. Further finely wrought translations by Tomlinson, in collaboration with Henry G. Gifford, have appeared in *Castilian Ilexes: Versions from Antonio Machado* (Oxford: Oxford University Press, 1963).

Ben Belitt, following his vigorous conviction that translation should be cast into an equivalent but also self-contained mould, has given us five selections from the songbook of Abel Martín, published as an appendix to *Juan de Mairena: Epigrams, Maxims, Memoranda, and Memoirs of an Apocryphal Professor,* ed. and trans. Ben Belitt (Berkeley: University of California Press, 1963).

# III

# Juan Ramón Jiménez

---

## The Religion of Poetry

To see a world in a grain of sand
And a heaven in a wild flower,
Hold infinity in the palm of your hand
And eternity in an hour.
            William Blake,
      "Auguries of Innocence"

# The Art of Being Dedicated

The reader of Juan Ramón Jiménez gradually begins to feel a certain uneasiness. This world the poet has created —a world of delicate beauty and pristine forms—is certainly not of the present time and place, the implacable here and now of the human condition.

Slowly the uneasiness becomes a sense of guilt, the cause of which is twofold. We first inquire for minimum evidence that this man had lived through two world wars, including the civil tragedy of his own country which produced half a million dead. Is there a trace of the fact that the last fifteen years of his life, he, like all of us, lived under the ominous billows of the mushroom cloud? But not only has Juan Ramón Jiménez transcended the brutality of history; he has also banished the vulgarity of routine existence from his verse. And this is the second source of our guilt feeling, for a great deal of contemporary poetry has successfully been concerned with incorporating everyday reality into verse. Richard Wilbur writes of a clothesline full of wash in Rome, and Marianne Moore, in the amazing crucible of her mind, can convert such mundane items as insects, toads, and steamrollers into the stuff of poetry.

The fact that we are uneasy with Jiménez' poetry is a disturbing commentary on our times. We have been conditioned by the especially peremptory nature of modern history, and by critics like Sartre, to suspect literature for its own sake. We wonder if Jiménez working in his cork-lined study, shielded from the basic

*contretemps* of existence by his devoted wife, ever really "lived";
and by asking the question we betray our own ignorance of living.

These reflections underline the difficulty in approaching
Jiménez' creation. His world of refinement and sensitivity is
ultimately a spiritual world that exists for its own sake. We are
so used to demanding practicality that we forget the world of
pure essence. But Jiménez was wedded to it. After an early affair
with *modernismo* and the *albo lirio* (white lily) of sensualism,
he devoted his entire energy and talent to exploring the essence
of poetry. In the end, this led him to a consideration of the
creative process itself, and much of his best final poetry is a
metaphor of the creative human mind.

His preciosity, especially apparent in translation which cannot preserve the niceties of distinction, is something we must
put up with, like Wordsworth's lapses of taste or Yeats's private cosmogony. For Jiménez at his best is a very great poet—
one who expanded the limits of the Spanish language and
created a new idiom. In his world of subtle relationships, the
most important question is:

> ¿Sostiene la hoja seca
> a la luz que la encanta,
> o la luz
> a la hoja encantada?
> (p. 658)[1]

> Does the dry leaf nourish
> the light that enchants it,
> or the light
> the enchanted leaf?

The same question was formulated by Yeats: "How can we
know the dancer from the dance?" Art is concerned with point-

1. Unless otherwise indicated, all quotations are from *Tercera antolojía poética*
(*1898–1953*) (Madrid: Biblioteca Nueva, 1957). I should like to thank Francisco H.-Pinzón Jiménez for permission to use Jiménez' poems, and the University of Texas Press, publisher of Eloïse Roach's anthology, *Three Hundred
Poems, 1903–1953*, for permission to include in the present volume translations
of poems for which it holds the English-language rights.

ing up such relationships, for every successful work of art is a splendid identification of form and content, of dancer and dance, of light and leaf—moulded into a moment of enchantment.

To create and explore these moments was the task that Jiménez daily set himself, from middle age until his death. He pursued his objective exclusively, ridding himself of all distractions. Art was his religion, and religion is kept alive by meditation and solitude. Juan Ramón's zealously maintained isolation was due to a deep need to refute the absurdity of existence, to retreat from the desperate farce of the world into the inner realm which alone provided undistorted experience. The process is known in Hindu and Buddhist philosophies as *viveka*, "discrimination."[2]

Jiménez was as deeply involved in the problem of life as any disciple of Sartre struggling in the rattrap of the universe; his vantage point was simply different. Those who criticize him as being divorced from the reality of the human condition should note the amazing humanistic basis of his final mystic poetry. His flight soared upward from the earth, but he never ceased to underscore the dark veins of clay that gave him being. As he paradoxically put it, one must have "roots that fly."

Some of Juan Ramón's final remarks concerning poetry, as recorded by Ricardo Gullón, provide an excellent summary of a lifetime's work. "Poetry," he said to Gullón, "is an attempt to approximate the absolute by means of symbols. Universality is

2. Joseph Campbell, *The Hero with a Thousand Faces* (New York: Meridian, 1956), pp. 17–18. Ricardo Gullón has taken great pains to vindicate Jiménez' aloofness toward society, an effort of special significance in Spain, where the current trend of social realism in poetry ignores Jiménez. Gullón reminds us that Juan Ramón sustained a vast correspondence with other writers, founded reviews, taught, and demonstrated a continuing interest in beginning poets—all of which does not suggest a man lacking in humanity. See "Juan Ramón en su laberinto," *Insula*, XII, Nos. 128–29 (1957), p. 6. The metaphysical urge innate in Jiménez' need for seclusion can be appreciated in the context of Alfred Kazin's remark concerning William Blake, a poet whom Jiménez much admired. Blake's withdrawal from society, said Kazin, was due to an ". . . unappeasable longing for the absolute integration of man, in his total nature, with the universe" (*The Inmost Leaf* [New York: Harcourt, Brace, 1955], p. 38).

personal—the essence of each one elevated to the absolute. . . . Poetry in its conception should be sacred, winged, and full of grace, and the proper realm of poetry is mystery and enchantment."[3]

To follow Jiménez in his search for the absolute is a task immensely complicated by his prolixity. He published some thirty books and had material for one hundred and fifty more. He wrote about six thousand poems and ten thousand aphorisms, one of the latter every day of his adult life. In his last years, he viewed with remorse this fecundity, for his ruthless critical sense told him that he could never cull for posterity the best of such an enormous creative outpouring; he would never live that long.

The approach to this vast canon, however, can be facilitated by dividing it into three main periods: melancholy impressionism; the search for beauty and the struggle with time; the encounter with absolute beauty or eternity. In distinguishing these epochs, we must keep in mind, as he did, the ultimate goal of his labors: the need for an absolute experience, the desire that his total human nature should transcend the limits of time and space. This goal assumed many names during his long career: sensual pleasure, nature, excellence, love, beauty, and finally the spirit of creativity, that sacred craft of the human mind. But whatever the rubric, the aim was always identical; after a few hesitant turns, Jiménez settled on his course and wrote with an unremitting sense of purpose for the rest of his days.

*Water Lilies* (*Ninfeas*) and *Violet Souls* (*Almas de violeta*), both published in 1900, are his first books. They are strongly marked by Rubén Darío's *modernismo,* as well as a general sense of *fin de siècle* malaise. He quickly freed himself of this influence, exhibited most disagreeably in a cloying morbidity, and began the characteristic effort to refine his perceptions, all the while experimenting with new techniques. In *Pastorales,* written from 1903 to 1905, he also broke with the forms of

---

3. *Conversaciones con Juan Ramón Jiménez* (Madrid: Taurus, 1958), p. 108, hereafter referred to as *Conversaciones.*

*modernismo* and used the traditional ballad meter. Despite uncertainty and a return to despondency under the influence of Baudelaire in *Laberinto* (1910–11), he reached the height of his first period with *Spiritual Sonnets* (*Sonetos espirituales,* 1914–15) and *Summer* (*Estío,* 1915).[4] During these years, his reading consisted mainly of Bécquer, the *romances,* the French symbolists, and Heine.

The year 1916 is one of change, marking the beginning of Jiménez' intermediate period. He went to America and married there. His encounter with the sea produced a great restlessness which, in turn, resulted in one of the most remarkable books of Spanish poetry, first published in 1917 under the title of *Diary of a Newly Married Poet* (*Diario de un poeta recién casado*), and republished in 1948 as *Diary of Poet and Sea* (*Diario de poeta y mar*), a title which more aptly describes the contents.

Obsessed by the idea of concentration, of seeking more avidly the perfect poem, he edited, in 1922, his famous *Second Poetic Anthology* (*Segunda antolojía poética*), and wrote *Rock and Sky* (*Piedra y cielo,* 1917–18), as well as the marvelous twin volumes of 1917–23, called *Poesía* (*en verso*) and *Belleza* (*en verso*): poetry and beauty—in verse.

The third period embraces his residence in America, occasioned by the Spanish Civil War. His desire for perfection finally led him to a highly particular form of mysticism, his logical goal from the outset. The best Spanish poetry is fated to be mystical, with or without a god, he averred in 1941.[5] During an ocean voyage to Buenos Aires in 1948, he wrote *Animal of Depth* (*Animal de fondo*), a triumphant celebration of his life's work.

One cannot forbear mentioning, even in a discussion of poetry, his exquisite prose achievements. *Platero and I* (*Platero y yo*), published in 1917, is undoubtedly his most widely known

---

4. Throughout this discussion of Jiménez, dates refer to the time of composition, unless otherwise indicated.

5. Quoted in Donald F. Fogelquist, "Juan Ramón Jiménez: Vida y obra," *Revista Hispánica Moderna,* XXIV (1958), 169, n. 67.

book. Its impressions of the world of an Andalusian donkey are, in effect, pure poetry. The *Diary of Poet and Sea* contains some of the most original prose pages in contemporary Spanish, and *Spaniards of Three Worlds* (*Españoles de tres mundos*), brought out in 1942, is a penetrating and subjective collection of literary portraits.

His labors were crowned with the Nobel Prize for Literature in 1956. The death of his wife a few days afterwards mingled with the pleasure a despair from which he never recovered. Their relationship was basic to his life and work, and will receive special attention later.

When death overtook him, he was planning a general edition of his works under the title "Destiny." *Animal of Depth* was to be part of a larger work entitled *God Desired and Desiring* (*Dios deseado y deseante*), of which some poems had already appeared.

With this general outline to serve us, we shall follow him in his quest for the grail, tracing the strands of duality, studying various themes concentric to the main one, and seeing his ideas come together at last in the "total center."

## The Melancholy Impressionist

"The afternoon succumbed in idealisms. . . ."
*Tercera antolojía poética*, p. 23

Refinement, grace, and lyricism are characteristics of Andalusian poets. Juan Ramón was born December 23, 1881, in Moguer, a small town in southwestern Andalusia, near the blue bays and pine groves which bade good-by to Columbus. In this peaceful, lovely environment he grew up. The indigo skies, the brown streets with their white houses, and the ancient layers of civilization—from Phoenician to Arabic—contributed to his formation. Like that other Andalusian, Antonio Machado, he carried the stamp of his native region into the greater world.

When he arrived in Madrid in 1900, he was a youth with disturbingly dark eyes and a morbid nature. Rubén Darío and

Francisco Villaespesa helped him launch his first two books. They welcomed one who was briefly but truly a *modernista*. Juan Ramón later vehemently disowned these inaugural volumes, but he paid constant homage to the movement they represent, a broad tendency toward change, of which he was a product. He qualified the influence of Darío, however. Both he and Machado, he recalled, made the acquaintance of Verlaine in the original, not through Darío.[6]

A perusal of these first slim volumes proves somewhat embarrassing today. They exaggerate his morbidity and rejection of society. Yet, although we react unfavorably to the excessive preoccupation with the demise of children and virgins, we can also see therein the kernel of a basic theme: the fate of beauty. And if his petulant espousal of sadness leaves us initially unmoved, we soon find it woven with genuine feeling into the remainder of his youthful works. Melancholy was a ruling emotion of his life and not a mere pose. He did not begin to transcend it until middle age and did not triumph over it until his final years.

For Juan Ramón was moved by beauty, and beauty was fleeting. He sought purity and encountered stains. Furthermore, no one seemed to mind. "The sadness so apparent in my poetry," he remarked in *Spaniards of Three Worlds*, "has never been related to its truest motive: the anguish of the adolescent, the young man, and the mature person who feels himself unattached and alone in his vocation."[7] At best, everything was surrounded by a vague sadness or nostalgia:

> ...¡Qué triste es amarlo todo,
> sin saber lo que se ama!
>
> (p. 35)

6. His antipathy towards his first books was so strong that he resorted to unscrupulous means in order to destroy as many copies as he could. Friends would be charged with the task of borrowing them from libraries and replacing the text with other pages (*Conversaciones*, p. 80). For the precedence of Verlaine over Darío, see *ibid.*, pp. 56, 102.

7. Quoted in Ricardo Gullón, "Vivir en poesía," *Clavileño*, VII, No. 42 (1956), p. 18.

...How sad it is to love everything,
without knowing what is loved!

Eventually, he recognized that the sadness of isolation was the crucible of his verse:

¡Siempre, después, qué contento
cuando me quedo conmigo!
¡Lo que iba a ser mi minuto,
fue, corazón, mi infinito!
(p. 589)

Always, afterwards, how content
when I remain with myself!
What was to be my minute
became, O heart, my infinity!

Nature, in particular, gave him cause for sweet sadness, and his early contemplation of the natural world was the beginning of a long, complex, and loving relationship. He took from nature nearly all the metaphors and images which embellish his art.[8] The *Second Anthology,* in which he assembled the highlights of twenty years of writing, opens with a poem to dawn. He cherished flowers, considering them the most expressive of gifts, and his love of the stars made him an avid reader of books about astronomy. Often the superb brilliance of a certain day would thoroughly overcome him: "How fearful the blue of the sky!" (p. 299).

He heard most frequently the still, sad music emanating from woods and fields as they pass through their endless cycle. From a few examples of the many poems devoted to this theme, we may comprehend something of his early response to one of the chief elements of his art:

Mi alma es hermana del cielo
gris y de las hojas secas.
¡Sol interno del otoño,
pásame con tu tristeza!

—Los árboles del jardín
están cargados de niebla.

8. Fogelquist, "Juan Ramón Jiménez," p. 127, n. 10.

Mi corazón ve por ellos
esa novia que no encuentra;
y en el suelo húmedo me abren
sus manos las hojas secas.
¡Si mi alma fuera una hoja
y se perdiera entre ellas!—

El sol ha mandado un rayo
de oro extraño a la arboleda,
un rayo flotante, dulce
luz a las cosas secretas.

—¡Qué ternura tiene el último
sol para las hojas secas!
Una armonía sin fin
vaga por todas las sendas,
lenta, eterna sinfonía
de músicas y de escencias,
que dora el jardín de una
más divina primavera—.

Y esa luz de bruma y oro,
que pasa las hojas secas,
irisa en mi corazón
no sé qué ocultas bellezas.

(pp. 45-46)

My soul is sister to the grey
sky and the dry leaves.
Inner sun of autumn,
pass through me with your sadness!

—The trees in the garden
are heavy with fog.
My heart sees among them
the lover it cannot find;
and in the wet soil dry leaves
spread their hands before me.
Oh, that my soul were a leaf
and lost among them!—

The sun has sent a ray
of strange gold to the grove,
a floating ray, sweet
light to secret things.

—What tenderness the last sun
has for the dry leaves!

An endless harmony
wanders on every path,
slow, eternal symphony
of music and essences,
illuminating the garden
in a diviner spring—.

And the light of mist and gold,
entering the dry leaves
ignites in my heart
an unknown hidden beauty.

Underlying the poem is a basic desire to identify: "My soul is sister to the grey / sky . . ."; "Oh, that my soul were a leaf. . . ." Clearly, the agent of identification is the light, not a strong, piercing one, but the muted glow of a sad autumn sun. When it enters the poet's heart, it brings with it the harmony that had been wandering outside. All of Juan Ramón's life is an effort to identify with these secret things, and his sadness is due to being excluded. When the light shines in the divine radiance of his final phase, the moments of epiphany will dispel all sorrow.

Arrival of light, banishing the uneasy fear of night, is the motif of the following poem. It is written in ballad meter and represents a definite break with *modernismo:*

(...anda el agua de alborada...
*Romance popular*)

Doraba la luna el río
—¡fresco de la madrugada!—
Por el mar venían olas
teñidas de luz de alba.

El campo débil y triste
se iba alumbrando. Quedaba
el canto roto de un grillo,
la queja oscura de un agua.

Huía el viento a su gruta,
el horror a su cabaña;
en el verde de los pinos
se iban abriendo las alas.

Las estrellas se morían,
se rosaba la montaña;
allá en el pozo del huerto,
la golondrina cantaba.

(p. 96)

(...flows the morning water...
*Popular ballad*)

The moon turned gold the river
—coolness of early morn!—
From the sea came waves
tinged by the light of dawn.

The sad, weak fields
came aglow. The broken song
of the cricket remained,
the dark cry of water.

The wind fled to its cave,
horror to its cabin;
in the green of the pines
wings were opening.

The stars were dying,
the mountain turning pink;
there in the garden well,
the swallow was singing.

The ballad is the father of this simple declamatory style.
Gone is the wavering, impressionistic touch that provided the
basis for the description of the autumn sun in the earlier poem
analyzed above. Instead, Jiménez reveals the sure arrival of
dawn by using the imperfect tense, a verb form that emphasizes
gradual or continued movement. (The constant translation of
this tense into its English equivalent would be clumsy, and I
have avoided doing so here.) The subtle music is impossible to
re-create. The first line is so perfectly natural that, by inverting
verb and subject, it could become prose, yet it is pure music.
The juxtaposition of opposing elements is not as skillful as it
will later be, but the use of "dark cry," "horror," and "cave"
suggests a deeply rooted emotion (melancholy?) that is tem-

porarily forced to flee by the arrival of daylight. Wings are
associated with light and will develop into a common symbol
for it.

Thus, early sadness was mixed with a profound comfort
derived from nature. Certainly, Juan Ramón's only true moments of peace were discovered in communion with natural
elements, when he could hear the world turning and feel Bethle-
hem descending to every stable (pp. 353–54). As he ap-
proached middle age, this peace settled deep into his fiber, and he
achieved, at least on the level of ordinary pantheism, the identification he was seeking in the autumn landscape of his youth.
It is instructive to compare the following consummate poem
on autumn, taken from the *Spiritual Sonnets* (1914–15), with
the first one quoted. We may see how far he came along the
ascending path of purification:

### Otoño

Esparce octubre, al blando movimiento
del sur, las hojas áureas y las rojas,
y, en la caída clara de sus hojas,
se lleva al infinito el pensamiento.

¡Qué noble paz en este alejamiento
de todo; oh prado bello, que deshojas
tus flores; oh agua, fría ya, que mojas
con tu cristal estremecido el viento!

¡Encantamiento de oro! ¡Cárcel pura,
en que el cuerpo, hecho alma, se enternece,
echado en el verdor de una colina!

En una decadencia de hermosura,
la vida se desnuda, y resplandece
a escelsitud de su verdad divina.

(p. 432)

### Autumn

October scatters, to a soft movement
from the south, red and golden leaves,
and, in their clear falling,
carries thought to infinity.

What noble peace in this withdrawal
of everything; O lovely field, plucking
your flowers; O water, now cold, wetting
the wind with trembling crystal!

Enchantment of gold! Pure prison,
where the body, become soul, tenderly
lies on the greenness of the hill!

In a beautiful descent,
life is uncovered and shines
from the loftiness of its divine truth.

The sad golden light evoked earlier by the poet has passed
through him and related his thought to infinity. One of the
themes of the poem is the uncovering of life's divine nature as
glimpsed in the beautiful dying of fall. The dual concept of
laying bare and dying is sustained throughout by the felicitous
use of the verb *caer* (to fall). Falling leaves are beautiful in
themselves (*caída clara*), but they also expose life's vulnerabil-
ity, the process of change that Jiménez accepts as a divine truth.
The poem is not without its ambiguity, the same we feel before
the splendor of autumn. *Decadencia* represents the notion of
falling, but it also can mean "decline" or "decadence." By join-
ing it with the phrase *de hermosura*, Jiménez bridges the gap
between beauty and change and helps make possible the strong
note of tranquillity that marks his sonnet.

In the subtle interplay between wind and water in the second
stanza, Jiménez has brilliantly projected his favorite problem:
the relation of the individual to the universe. At the moment
there seems to be a perfect interaction without loss of identity.
Water wets the wind yet trembles because of the wind. The
interaction foresees the reciprocal character of the "god desired
and desiring" that he will discover toward the close of his life.

With this serene orchestration of the elements of nature and
the human spirit, we have arrived at the peak of Juan Ramón's
treatment of nature in his first phase.

The nagging lack of identity we noticed in these nature
poems has many ramifications:

¿Soy yo quien anda, esta noche,
por mi cuarto, o el mendigo
que rondaba mi jardín,
al caer la tarde?...
                              Miro
en torno y hallo que todo
es lo mismo y no es lo mismo...
¿La ventana estaba abierta?
¿Yo no me había dormido?
¿El jardín no estaba verde
de luna?... El cielo era limpio
y azul... Y hay nubes y viento
y el jardín está sombrío...
Creo que mi barba era
negra... Yo estaba vestido
de gris... Y mi barba es blanca
y estoy enlutado... ¿Es mío
este andar? ¿Tiene esta voz
que ahora suena en mí los ritmos
de la voz que yo tenía?
¿Soy yo, o soy el mendigo
que rondaba mi jardín
al caer la tarde?...

                              (pp. 73-74)


Is it I walking tonight
through my room, or the beggar
who roamed my garden
as afternoon came down?...
                              I gaze
about and find that everything
is the same and is not the same...
Was the window open?
Had I not fallen asleep?
Was the garden not green
from the moon?... The sky was clear
and blue... And there are clouds and wind
and the garden is somber...
I think my beard was
black... I was dressed
in grey... And my beard is white
and I am in mourning... Is this
my step? Does this voice

now sounding in me have the rhythm
of the voice I had?
Is it I, or am I the beggar
who roamed my garden
as afternoon came down?...

The confusion stems as much from the technique of impressionism as it does from a search for identity. If for the impressionist no phenomenon is ever the same, no color is equal to what it was a second ago, then impressionism in this poem has reached the level of personality. Not only do things change, but also the onlooker, aggravating the difficulty of identification. The beggar symbolizes Jiménez' quest, his petition for wholeness, for knowledge of himself and beauty.

Identification with people was, of course, impossible. The barrier of general insensibility thoroughly distressed him and made him suspicious of his fellow men; at the same time, he strongly believed that the problem of identification must be solved within the bounds of each individual's loneliness. Over and over again, the word *nadie* (no one) appears, usually in conjunction with landscape: "streets with no one" (p. 237); "how fine with no one!" (p. 317). Water, flowers, and wind usurp the rôle of people: "Is the water not some one?" (p. 75). Persons present are types, such as cart drivers, sailors, farmers; or they are generic children and women. Only rarely does a definite personality appear.

Within this situation of isolation and shifting forms, love holds a unique place. Like everything else in the early lyrics, it is imbued with sadness:

> ¿Para qué, aquella tarde,
> enlutada de blanco,
> entre risas y lágrimas,
> me besaste en la tierra?
> ¿Para qué? ¡Quién lo sabe!
> ¿Para darme tristeza?
>
> (p. 26)

> Why that afternoon,
> robed in white mourning,

between laughter and tears,
did you kiss me on the earth?
Why? Who knows!
To make me sad?

But this sadness is related only to specific affairs. Loving a particular woman did not cause his melancholy to abate; however, womankind as a symbol of beauty, the eternal loved one, was the essence of what he was striving to know, and as such was akin to nature:

Bajo al jardín. ¡Son mujeres!
¡Espera, espera!... Mi amor
coje un brazo. ¡Ven! ¿Quién eres?
¡Y miro que es una flor!

¡Por la fuente; sí, son ellas!
¡Espera, espera, mujer!
...Cojo el agua. ¡Son estrellas,
que no se pueden cojer!

                                        (p. 67)

I go down to the garden. They are women!
Wait, wait!... My desire
grasps an arm. Come! Who are you?
And I see it is a flower!

By the fountain; yes, it is they!
Wait, wait, woman!
...I grasp the water. It is stars,
which cannot be held.

The marked sensuality of Jiménez' early poetry was soon suppressed or, more accurately, channeled into his consuming desire to transcend. Within a single poem we often find incompatible concepts, such as "the vain, soft roundness of your breasts" and "the ineffable net of our thoughts" (p. 228). Human love is victimized by the ever-present dichotomy of body and soul. The flesh is readily known, but the mind presses for more. The following poem is symbolic of this frustration, and also shows why the pleasure of the senses must take on added dimensions:

No te he tenido más en mí,
que el río tiene al árbol de la orilla;
yo, pasando, me estaba siempre en tu alma;
tú, estando en mi alma siempre, nunca te venías...
Bastaba un cielo ciego, un pobre viento,
para que desaparecieras de mi vida.

(p. 405)

I have had you no more in me
than the river possesses the tree on its shore;
flowing by, I was always in your soul;
being always in my soul, you never came...
A blind sky, some poor wind sufficed
to banish you from my life.

Jiménez never renounced the flesh; he merely stated its limitations. His quixotic desire was to unite the physical and spiritual world. Thus, as we shall see, his mysticism is not a sublimation of the flesh but a celebration of it, an effort to make it as timeless as the spirit. The reader soon notices the abundant use of the pronouns *tú* (you) and *ella* (she), and realizes that they rapidly cease to refer to the poet's dark-eyed fleeting loves, the stereotyped *modernista* ladies of fascinating flesh and moribund languor. The love affair alluded to in the following poem has overtones that place it beyond a transitory tryst:

Para quererte, al destino
le he puesto mi corazón.
¡Ya no podrás libertarte
—¡ya no podré libertarme!—
de lo fatal de este amor!

No lo pienso, no lo sientes;
yo y tú somos ya tú y yo,
como el mar y como el cielo
cielo y mar, sin querer, son.

(p. 436)

In order to love you, I have
commended my heart to destiny.
You can no longer escape
—I can no longer escape!—
the fate of this love!

I do not think it, you do not feel it;
I and you are now you and I,
as the sea and the sky
cannot help being sky and sea.

The union portrayed in the last stanza is transcendental. Jiménez conceived of love as an urge to know the universe, an emanation of self to the world:

Subes de ti misma,
como un surtidor
de una fuente.
            No
se sabe hasta dónde
llegará tu amor,
porque no se sabe
dónde está el venero
de tu corazón.

—Eres ignorada,
eres infinita,
como el mundo y yo.—
                        (p. 438)

You flow from yourself
like the jet
of a fountain.
            It
is not known how far
your love will reach,
for no one knows
where the wellspring
of your heart is.

—You are unknown,
you are infinite,
just as the world and I.—

From now on, love will be stated in these ecumenical terms: the world and I and beauty. It is a relationship best symbolized by the union of sea and sky—something immense, delicate, and without definition. *Tú* and *ella* become the pronouns for this relationship, the surrogates of love, flame, flower, music, light, perfection: in summation, the poet's quest. Jiménez was partially guided in his search for the absolute by the conviction that there did exist a platonic archetype, an ideal norm which he could know by means of poetry. In "The Spike of Wheat" ("La espiga"), written during 1910 and 1911, he celebrated the ritual of planting and harvest—of entering into the ground to grow again—and in the final stanza proclaimed the motive for this cycle:

> Y... ¡otra vez a la tierra! Anhelo inestinguible,
> ante la norma única de la espiga perfecta,
> de una suprema forma, que eleve a lo imposible
> el alma, ¡oh poesía!, infinita, áurea, recta!
>
> (p. 211)

> And... once again to the earth! Unquenchable desire
> before the unique norm of the perfect spike of wheat,
> a supreme form that will raise the soul
> to impossible poetry, infinite, golden, erect!

A favorite symbol for the "unique norm" is the rose. The poet himself must become, like the rose, "all essence" (p. 315), in order to apprehend perfection; his soul is a branch, constantly ready to sustain the perfect rose. Once he has prepared himself, his creation will be "the norm of roses" (p. 427). A second common symbol of perfection is the star, variously presented as light or gold; it is the medium by which his soul is purified. Finally, woman symbolizes the incarnation of beauty. In *The Total Season* (*La estación total*), published in 1946, he acclaimed his trinity: "woman, star, and rose, / the three most beautiful forms in the world."[9]

His achievement at the age of thirty-four is nicely summarized in the following sonnet:

> Nada
>
> A tu abandono opongo la elevada
> torre de mi divino pensamiento.
> Subido a ella, el corazón sangriento
> verá la mar, por él empurpurada.
>
> Fabricaré en mi sombra la alborada,
> mi lira guardaré del vano viento,

9. *La estación total* (Buenos Aires: Losada, 1946), p. 139.

buscaré en mis entrañas mi sustento...
Mas ¡ay!, ¿y si esta paz no fuera nada?

   ¡Nada, sí, nada, nada!... —O que cayera
mi corazón al agua, y de este modo
fuese el mundo un castillo hueco y frío...—

   Que tú eres tú, la humana primavera,
la tierra, el aire, el agua, el fuego, ¡todo!
...¡y soy yo sólo el pensamiento mío!

(p. 418)

### Nothing

   To your neglect I oppose the elevated
tower of my divine thought.
Once ascended, my bleeding heart
will view the sea it has made purple.

   I shall create the dawn in my shadow,
my lyre guard from the vain wind,
in my vitals I shall seek my sustenance...
But, alas, if this peace be nothingness?

   Nothing, yes, nothing at all!... —Or if
my heart should fall into the water, and thus
the world become a cold and hollow castle...—

   For you are you, the human springtime,
earth, air, water, fire—all!
...and I am only these thoughts of mine!

This sonnet portrays an important stage in Jiménez' struggle
for wholeness. Since spirit and matter refuse to be welded together ("A tu abandono . . ."), he must build a tower of divine
thought. (The tower commonly suggests contemplation; compare Milton's "Il Penseroso": "Or let my lamp, at midnight
hour, / Be seen in some high lonely tower.") From this tower,
Jiménez can inform the world lying about him like a sea. He will
plumb his "vitals," searching for material from which to create
beauty. Unfortunately, there is the strong possibility that the
tower (i.e., art and contemplation) is an illusion. Also, death
waits outside. The final tercet reveals the dichotomy—the
world without and the world within. The title suggests the
pointlessness of thought that is not nourished by reality.

Jiménez' style deserves special comment, for he was one of the great craftsmen in the language, constantly rewriting and editing. He attached so much importance to the correction of a poem that he christened the process "re-creation."[10]

The style of his early poetry was inspired by French symbolism and impressionism. To this effect, he employed elliptical phrases, made liberal use of questions, and was fond of interpolation. His general plan was to comply with the injunction of the symbolists: suggest rather than state. "Describe not the object itself, but the effect it produces," went Mallarmé's famous maxim.[11] Jiménez' questions delicately pose an effect, avoiding bald declaration:

> Su canto enajena.
> —¿Se ha parado el viento?—
> (p. 140)

> Its song enraptures.
> Has the wind stopped?—

The question implies that the beauty of the bird's song is so compelling that the wind has respectfully ceased its own music. The use of elliptical constructions was an additional means— much overworked—of suggesting rather than describing. We are often required to complete phrases such as the following: "The going away of the path..." (p. 31).

For a writer committed to sifting every shred of experience, interpolation was as necessary as breathing. No sooner was one thought expressed than a ramification or an opposite would

---

10. Jiménez was constantly annoyed by printing errors. He would threaten to stop contributing to magazines when they published his poems minus a comma or a dash. During World War II, he recorded broadcasts to Latin America for Nelson Rockefeller. He readily admitted the need for military censorship, but refused to permit any last-minute cuts to tailor the program to time. He was adamant until Henry Wallace arranged that he be allowed to see these changes (*Conversaciones*, p. 47). Similarly, he developed strong ideas about orthography, believing that it should be more phonetic. This involved, among other things, the substitution of *j* for *g* before the vowels *i* and *e*, and *s* for *x* before consonants. His spelling has been respected in this study.

11. Mallarmé: *Selected Prose Poems*, trans. Brad Cook (Baltimore, Md.: Johns Hopkins Press, 1956), p. 83.

suggest itself. Thus, a considerable portion of Jiménez' poetry is largely a series of quotes within quotes, the method he used to interpolate another facet or a different perspective into the body of the poem. The interpolation may be quite short—an adjective, as if in afterthought, which suddenly adds a new dimension—or it may be an entire concept, occupying as much as a whole stanza. "Nada" is a good example of the extensive use of interpolation.

Another technique inherited from symbolism is synaesthesia, the association of disparate senses:

> ¡Quiero cantar, y no sé qué! No es de palabras
> esta esplosión aguda que en el corazón siento;
> son aromas que suenan bien, llantos que huelen
> bien, son májicos ojos que se espresan con ecos...
>
> (p. 285)

> I want to sing I know not what! There are no words
> for this sharp explosion I feel in my heart;
> it is of fine-sounding aromas, weeping that smells
> good, magic eyes expressed with echoes...

The indiscriminate mixture of the senses is part of the effort to savor all possible angles of an experience; eyes that hear and feel, as well as see, would be the supreme endowment for a poet.

Among the early stylistic devices, the one with deepest implications is that of fluctuation (*vaivén*). It is also the device most constantly utilized throughout his entire work. In Jiménez' poems, everything comes and goes, nothing seems to be defined exactly in time or space (or, if it is, there is an immediate interpolation of a new aspect). Partly this is commensurate with the vague malaise, the amorphous sense of indisposition, characterizing his youth. Partly, also, it is his unwillingness to select any one experience as typical when his kaleidoscope shows him literally thousands of other brilliant patterns. Thus, things are always both near and far away, great and small, ethereal and concrete. But this apparent imprecision is in reality a mania for exactness and responds, as do all the impressionistic techniques, to his wish to describe all aspects of reality and thereby tran-

scend it. The creative process, by its imperfections, adumbrated
the possibilities he sought:

> ¿Cómo pondré en la hora
> tu vago sentimiento?
>
> ¡Hacia la aurora! ¡Más!
> ¡Hacia el ocaso! ¡Menos!
>
> Siempre le falta un poco...
> Le sobra siempre un dedo...
>
> —Tu reír suena, fino,
> muy cerca... desde lejos.—
>
> (p. 437)
>
> How shall I place in time
> your vague sensation?
>
> Towards the dawn! More!
> Towards the sunset! Less!
>
> Always a bit is lacking...
> There is always a touch too much...
>
> —Your laughter sounds lightly,
> very close... from afar.—

In order to pin down this hovering presence, to capture the
subtle (but perhaps mocking) laughter, style would have to
become an overwhelming preoccupation. He was ready to succumb to the passion for the "exact word."

# Beauty versus Time: The Search for Eternity

> "For only one moment was your motion;
> but you remained, as in stone,
> moving forever."
> *Tercera antolojía poética*, p. 529

Ricardo Gullón has written that evolution in Jiménez is best
defined as a process of elimination.[12] For elimination,
read also purification. In the preface to *Diary of Poet and Sea,*
Jiménez states: "Never more different; always higher, the constant purification of the same thing. . . ."[13]

---

12. Gullón, "Vivir en poesía," p. 22.
13. *Diario de poeta y mar,* 2nd ed. (Madrid: Aguado, 1957), p. 10. All
references are to this edition.

From our present perspective on his work, it is a temptation to overemphasize its unity and consistently high quality. To correct this tendency, we should recall that Jiménez himself broke with his past, denouncing all that he had written through 1915 as a mere rough draft. The famous *Second Anthology,* which contains poems written from 1898 to 1918, is actually a rewriting of his youthful work. A comparison of the original version of some of these pieces with their final form in the *Second Anthology* demonstrates the sharp difference between the young sentimental impressionist and the mature self-controlled poet.

Two factors were responsible for transforming Jiménez' poetry. The first was his marriage. In 1912 he met Zenobia Camprubí Aymar, the daughter of a Spanish father and a Puerto Rican mother. Juan Ramón and Zenobia were married in New York City, March 2, 1916, and it was the beginning of forty years of love and companionship. Zenobia devoted the rest of her life to helping Juan Ramón prepare his soul for the "just rose." His unique independence was maintained chiefly through her, for she protected him from banality. Lover, secretary, chauffeur, nurse, and mother were rôles she played supremely well in his life. When the announcement was made to him of the Nobel Prize, he said simply that it belonged to her. She died a few days later of cancer, and he a few months afterward. Those who knew her eagerness and vitality, her self-sacrifice combined with natural happiness, have testified that she was the perfect foil for her husband's hyper-sensibility and melancholy. The pronouns *tú* and *ella* can justly refer to her as much as to absolute beauty:

> ¡Sólo tú, más que Venus,
> puedes ser
> estrella mía de la tarde,
> estrella mía del amanecer!
>                    (p. 1033)

> Only you, more than Venus,
> can be

> my star of the afternoon,
> my star of the first light.

Zenobia had been educated in America, and under her influence Juan Ramón's outlook was considerably broadened. She turned his attention to the poetry of England, the United States, and Germany. The reading of Shakespeare, Blake, Shelley, Browning, Emily Dickinson, Goethe, and Hölderlin took the place of French lyrics and gave him a greater intellectual perspective during the remainder of his life.

### THE NAKED SEA

"Today, sea, thy name is life."
    *Diario,* p. 204

The second factor that caused a change was the sea. When Jiménez boarded ship at Cádiz to sail for New York, he was keeping a double rendezvous with destiny. The ship was to carry him to his future wife and also provide an intimate encounter with a great natural force. The record of this voyage was first called the *Diary of a Newly Married Poet* (*Diario de un poeta recién casado*), but in 1948 was changed to *Diary of Poet and Sea.* Although love plays a significant part in the book, it is subordinate to the experience of the ocean, which is the leitmotif. The *Diary* has been hailed as the beginning of modern symbolism in Spanish poetry. In it, Jiménez used free verse for the first time (". . . due to the waves, to my not feeling firm and secure . . .").[14] And he considered it his best book.

Travel is an unsettling experience for the sensitive and meditative soul. Having thought a great deal about time, space, and reality, the voyager suddenly discovers himself in the grip of what was heretofore only a concept. Thrust upon him in all its force, literally clamoring for clarification, is the puzzle of the true nature of the relationship between man and the world. Since he was constantly preoccupied with such relationships, Jiménez found the very depths of his nature bestirred by this ocean voyage.

14. *Conversaciones,* p. 84.

The sea, therefore, became a riddle in creativity: how to incorporate it into his aesthetic outlook and thereby account for it in terms of his longing for spirituality. The immediate attraction was balanced by an aversion, for the sea was coldly and vastly independent, not sounding with the sweet chords of nature he had heard in his Spanish landscapes. In the end, he apprehended the image of his own mind in the ocean's rapidly changing, yet fixed, nature. Its fateful mutations would mould the rest of his work. When he again returned to the sea in 1948, it would carry him into his "third sea," the final mystical stage.

This process is traced in the *Diary,* which provides glimpses of all subsequent facets of Jiménez' career.

The book begins in Madrid. Uprooted, in motion towards the port of embarkation, the poet is dwelling passionately on his love. His soul is all awareness, his heart is all body, eager to respond to the love that is waiting. He passes through Moguer, the scene of his childhood, and for a moment is overcome by the reality of the past suddenly become here and now. Yet all is falling toward the sea, which, while he is on the edge of it, is as indescribable as woman.

He embarks, and the theme of love disappears almost at once, submerged for the time being in the depths of the imposing, gigantic body of water. Initially, the ocean appears to him as the personification of solitude, so dear to his way of being. Its waves come and go, like his fluctuating thoughts, in eternal knowing and unknowing. Everything is in the sea, and yet the sea seems to be without itself, lacking identification (*Diario,* p. 40). The solitude has no inner warmth. Stupified, Jiménez begins to rebel at the limitations of language. The sensation of something so imposing, incomprehensible, and separate from himself creates one of his new preoccupations: nomenclature— the art of choosing the exact word. Neither the sea, nor the sky, as characterized by the sea, has a name. Until he can learn the proper designation he cannot make the sea his own. Baptism (or creation) is an act of identification. The whole experience is, as we have said, a puzzle in creativity. In this sense of the inade-

quacy of words, giving rise to a need to purify the language, re-
sides much of the modern impact of Jiménez' verse, his kinship to Mallarmé and Valéry. In the early pages of the *Diary,*
he contents himself with frequent recourse to the word *todo*
(everything), one which comes easily from his past. More than a
desire for integration, it signifies his bewilderment. For the time
being, there will be no other experience. Strange, vast, aloof,
limitless, the sea offers itself as ultimate reality to be transformed into poetry.

Accompanying the wonder before this event of wind and wave
is the opposite reaction of distress and revulsion. One day,
during his endless pondering upon the water, the word *nada*
(nothingness) suddenly takes on perfect meaning, finding its
exact site, like a body in its grave (*Diario,* p. 48). Besides being
a reaction to the separateness of the sea and its lack of identity,
this feeling is also a realization of death. We can understand
why *todo* often equals *nada,* and why the sea depressed him,
especially on dark days when it seemed to be floating iron, or a
mirror pierced with nothingness (*Diario,* p. 58).

Throughout the voyage to America the aspects of his creative
struggle are evoked. The sea wrestles in order to find itself or
that he may find it (*Diario,* p. 52), and thereby fit it into his
creation. Never before has he encountered such a strong obsti-
nate image of the present in all its incomprehensibility. And
never again will the past have any meaning except in terms of
the present and himself.

One senses a sigh of relief when Jiménez touches land with
its stock of trusted names and metaphors. Yet the traveler,
having once moved forward, can never move back. A few days
after he reached port, he wrote the following poem in recognition of the deep change he was undergoing and in anticipation
of the direction he would pursue:

### Golfo

La nube—blanco cúmulo—recoge
el sol que no se ve, blanca.

Abajo, en sombra, acariciando

el pie desnudo de las rocas,
el mar, remanso añil.
                              Y yo.

　　Es el fin visto,
y es la nada de antes.
Estoy en todo, y nada es todavía
sino el puerto del sueño.

　　La nube—blanco cúmulo—recoge
el sol que no se ve, rosa.

                          A donde quiera
que llegue, desde aquí, será a aquí mismo.

　　Estoy ya en el centro
en donde lo que viene y lo que va
unen desilusiones
de llegada y partida.

　　La nube—blanco cúmulo—recoge
el sol que no se ve, roja...
                    (*Diario,* pp. 72–73)

### Gulf

　　The cloud—white cumulus—gathers
white from the hidden sun.

　　Below, in shadow, caressing
the naked foot of rocks,
the still indigo sea.
                              And I.

　　It is the seen conclusion,
and the nothingness of before.
I am in everything, and nothing yet exists
except the port of dreams.

　　The cloud—white cumulus—gathers
pink from the hidden sun.

                          Wherever
I arrive from here will be here again.

　　Now I am in the center
where what comes and goes
unites the disillusions
of arrival and departure.

　　The cloud—white cumulus—gathers
red from the hidden sun...

Within the framework of restrained impressionism—the cloud reflecting white, pink, and red—there is a moment of integration, an instant when the perennial coming and going has been joined, the fluctuation of reality pinned down in a center composed of the poet and the sea. From now on, all motion will return to this point: the poet receiving and creating his world. The emphatic repetition of the word *aquí* (here), endemic in his later writing, springs from this perception. *Here,* in the center (to be more fully defined), is the beginning and the end. At this stage, he is almost certain that the human being is not only the singer of reality but also its receptacle.

Love considered ideally is quite different from the intimate daily contact with another person that results from marriage. For the self-centered, isolated, and egotistical Juan Ramón, the adjustment must have presented more than the usual difficulties. "How hard it is / to arrive with you to myself . . ." (*Diario,* p. 82) is the beginning of a poem written in Boston. As a result of Zenobia's understanding disposition, Jiménez was able to retain his exalted concept of love, both in the physical and spiritual sense. In the *Diary* we find him working through his new personal relationship towards the familiar goal:

> Cuando, dormida tú, me echo en tu alma,
> y escucho, con mi oído
> en tu pecho desnudo,
> tu corazón tranquilo, me parece
> que, en su latir hondo, sorprendo
> el secreto del centro
> del mundo.
>
> > (*Diario,* p. 106)

> When, past your sleep, I plunge into your soul
> and listen, with my ear
> on your bare breast,
> to your quiet heart, it seems to me
> that in its deep beat I surprise
> the secret
> of the world's center.

The couple embarked in June for the return voyage to Spain.

Once again in the grip of movement, he responded to the sea in terms of the love he had found:

¡Desnudo!

¡Desnudo ya, sin nada
más que su agua sin nada!
¡Nada ya más!

Este es el mar.
¡Este era el mar, oh amor desnudo!
(*Diario,* p. 177)

Naked!

Now naked, with nothing
more than water with nothing!
Nothing now more!

This is the sea.
This was the sea, O naked love!

No longer to be feared, *nada* now stands for purity, simplicity, the truth of unadornment—principles he will impose upon the style of his poetry. The love that he heard with his ear to the bare breast of his beloved has helped him accept the sea. He feels it stirring in his soul and clarifying his being. Most important of all, he has found its name: "Today, sea, thy name is life" (*Diario,* p. 204).

Full tribute to the experience of his ocean voyage may be found in a single poem from which are drawn these expressive lines:

Hasta estas puras noches tuyas, mar, no tuvo
el alma mía, sola más que nunca,
aquel afán, un día presentido,
del partir sin razón.

Esta portada
de camino que enciende en ti la luna
con toda la belleza de sus siglos
de castidad, blancura, paz y gracia,
la contagia del ansia de su claro
movimiento.

.    .    .    .    .    .    .    .    .

así empezaba aquel comienzo, gana
celestial de mi alma
de salir, por su puerta, hacia su centro...

(*Diario,* pp. 191–92)

Until these pure nights of sea, this soul of mine,
more alone than ever, did not possess
that desire, once before sensed,
to depart without reason.
This portal
of roadway that the moon ignites in you
with all the beauty of centuries
of chastity, whiteness, peace, and grace,
affects me with contagious anxiety for its clear
movement.

. . . . . . . . .

thus was the beginning, celestial
need of my soul
to leave, through its door, to its center...

The mystical desire clearly apprehended in this poem dominates
the rest of his poetry, and will always be associated with the sea,
the most fruitful symbol of his life's work. In the constant
surging of the ocean, he recognized and understood more deeply
his own need to create.

## THE PRESENT TRUTH

Everything flows forth from the *Diary* like sunlight from its
source, bathing the ensuing books in a brilliant new light. All
the revelations of the ocean voyage are intensely pursued. At
this time also, the incessant correction, or re-creation, of past
work begins.

Overshadowing everything else was the problem of language.
For a man obsessed with defining relationships, describing exactly the interplay between his spirit and the world, the choice
of words was a paramount act. Already we saw in the *Diary* his
loss for words when confronted with the ocean. Now in the face
of poetry itself, he stood without weapons, and began a new
book called *Eternities* with a paraphrase of Goethe:

No sé con qué decirlo,
porque aún no está hecha
mi palabra.

(p. 507)

I know not how to say it,
because my word is still
unmade.

Preoccupation with the limitations of language is very characteristic of modern poetry. It is a preoccupation which has played
an important rôle in purifying the "language of the tribe," as
Mallarmé said poetry should do. The term "pure poetry" used
in connection with the work of poets who followed Mallarmé's
precept is often badly understood. Valéry, in discussing the matter, pointed out that everyday language is the product of a
shared disorder in life, and that it is the task of the poet to take
this base material and turn it into something highly suggestive
and delicate. So-called pure poetry, therefore, is simply more
intense poetry, and also more carefully written poetry. We must
not forget that Valéry lamented the lack of any system of composition in language comparable to that which music possesses,
and also that he thought it not impossible some day for poetry
to be written more systematically than heretofore.

Jiménez' phrase *poesía desnuda* (naked poetry) means essentially the same thing as Valéry's *poésie pure*. The Spaniard had
always before him the goal of the perfect poem, even though
he recognized, as did Valéry, that it was an ideal impossible to
attain. But the concentration and purification of language was
eminently feasible:

¡Intelijencia, dame
el nombre exacto de las cosas!
(p. 509)

Intelligence, give me
the exact name of things!

The "exact name of things" is the name which will create the
emotion of poetry. When this has been done, the pure poet will
let the poem stand in its simplicity, a gem in the dross of words:

¡No le toques ya más,
que así es la rosa!
(p. 569)

Don't touch it any more,
for thus is the rose!

During this period, Jiménez at times seemed to suggest that
the perfect poem was one without words:

¡Canción mía,
canta, antes de cantar; . . .
(p. 571)

Song of mine,
sing before singing; . . .

But here it is well to bear in mind Valéry's distinction between
poetry and a poem. We say, for example, that a landscape is
poetic. By this we refer to the feeling of excitement or enchantment caused by special qualities in the landscape. A poem is an
effort to express these feelings in words. Jiménez was clearly
thinking of this distinction when in 1923 he entitled one of his
books *Poetry (in Verse)*.

The transcendental urge to express himself as perfectly as
possible informs everything he wrote after his marriage, giving
his life a "permanent, contained haste" (p. 578). More and
more he came to realize, as Machado had said, that now is forever:

Quisiera que mi libro
fuese, como es el cielo por la noche,
todo verdad presente, sin historia.

Que, como él, se diera en cada instante,
todo, con todas sus estrellas; sin
que, niñez, juventud, vejez, quitaran
ni pusieran encanto a su hermosura inmensa.
(p. 623)

I should wish my book
to be, as is the sky at night,
all present truth without a history.

That like the sky it every instant give itself,
entirely, with all its stars;

without childhood, youth, old age taking
or adding enchantment to its immense beauty.

The "present truth" is in defiance of time. As he grew older,
the radius of the moment of apprehension narrowed and became
more intense: "The present is only a point of support or comparison, each time more brief . . ." (p. 859). But his concern
was that each moment should be timeless:

>            Mañana en el jardín
>
>          ¡El niñito dormido!
>
>          Mientras, cantan los pájaros,
>          y las ramas se mecen,
>          y el sol grande sonríe.
>
>            ¡En la sombra dorada
>          —¿un siglo o un instante?—
>          el niñito dormido
>          —fuera aún de la idea
>          de lo breve o lo eterno!—
>
>            Mientras, cantan los pájaros,
>          y las ramas se mecen,
>          y el sol grande sonríe.
>                            (p. 701)
>
>          Morning in the Garden
>
>          The small child asleep!
>
>          While the birds sing,
>          and the branches sway,
>          and the great sun smiles!
>
>          In the golden shadow
>          —a century or an instant?—
>          the small child asleep
>          —still outside the idea
>          of brevity or eternity!—
>
>          While the birds sing,
>          and the branches sway,
>          and the great sun smiles.

In the process of compiling these moments of truth, which
hopefully may become eternal, the sense of something constantly
escaping tantalizes him:

Mariposa de luz,
la belleza se va cuando yo llego
a su rosa.

Corro, ciego, tras ella...
La medio cojo aquí y allá...

¡Sólo queda en mi mano
la forma de su huida!

(p. 603)

Butterfly of light,
beauty flees when I come
to its rose.

Blindly I pursue it...
I half grasp it here and there...

In my hand remains only
the form of its flight!

As in many of Mallarmé's poems, absence suggests more than
presence. Juan Ramón's debt, however, is directly to Bécquer
and St. John of the Cross; in the former we read that inspiration
is like a fleeting butterfly, "leaving in the hands that wish to
detain it the gold dust of its wings,"[15] while, according to the
latter, poetry is like air: when you close your hand, it escapes.[16]

Most poets would have been content with the delicate stain
of gold dust on their hands, but Jiménez, of course, wanted the
impossible. In this middle period, that unreasonable desire to
go forth from himself, which he had perceived one night at sea,
became more and more dominant:

Nostaljia

¡Hojita verde con sol,
tú sintetizas mi afán;
afán de gozarlo todo,
de hacerme en todo inmortal!

(p. 614)

Nostalgia

Little green and sunny leaf,
you summarize my need;

15. *Obras completas* (Buenos Aires: Ed. Joaquín Gil, 1946), pp. 675–76.
16. Jorge Guillén, *Language and Poetry: Some Poets of Spain* (Cambridge,
Mass.: Harvard University Press, 1961), p. 89.

the urge to enjoy everything,
to become in all immortal!

Juan Ramón did not uncover the existence of any god or
governing principle in the fullness of nature, and consequently
pantheism is not an accurate term with which to describe his
feelings toward nature. At certain moments, he felt an urge to
become part of the unquestionable existence of sky and leaves
and earth, but his sense of his own identity was so sharp that one
feels he lacked the true pantheist's willingness to surrender himself:

### 21 de octubre

¡No sois vosotras, dulces, bellas ramas
rojas, las que os mecéis
al viento último; es mi alma!

(p. 707)

### October 21

It is not you, sweet, lovely branches
of red, who rock
in the late wind; it is my soul!

The self-pitying aspect of his youthful solitude changed radically. "The earth dreams. / I, awake, / am its only mind"
(p. 733). Solitude is now equated with alertness, with preparation for epiphany. Over and over again the image of the solitary,
erect singer (*de pie*), listening for the quiet rumors of beauty,
appears in his lines. He views himself as standing in the world
like a tree, mysterious and secure, rich in magic moments:

¡Qué bello este vivir siempre de pie
—¡belleza!—,
para el descanso eterno de un momento!

(p. 703)

How lovely this living erectly
—beauty!—,
for the eternal rest of a moment!

## DEATH, SLEEP, AND SHADOW

"Death and life were not
Till man made up the whole. . . ."
          Yeats, "The Tower"

The quest for beauty involved a struggle to overcome time, and time presented itself to man as proof of his end. In a brief autobiographical note, Jiménez wrote, ". . . the death of my father [1900] flooded my soul with dark worry. Suddenly one night I felt as if I were drowning; I fell to the floor. This attack repeated itself. I had a deep fear of sudden death." Later in 1905, ". . . preoccupation with death led me from rest homes, to doctors, to clinics."[17]

By middle age he was able, at least in terms of his art, to subdue this pathological preoccupation. Death and its twin images, sleep and shadow, occupy a considerable and controlled part of his books *Poetry* and *Beauty*. What had been an unreasonable fear became a brave dialogue. Throughout his life he continued to be subject to fits of depression, occasioned by his morbidity, but, on the whole, his work represents a triumph over dread.

In his rationalization of man's fate, there are marks of existentialism, unconscious though they may be. A moving reminiscence of Antonio Machado refers to the latter's ". . . living-dying [which] overcame the gap between these existences, paradoxically opposed, yet the only ones known to us; existences strongly united even though we . . . men persist in separating . . . them. . . ."[18] Recognition of this intimate relationship between life and death underlies many poems written between 1917 and 1923. There are conventional lines, such as "Death is merely / looking inward . . ." (p. 665); there is also an intimation that death is not absolute. But the most striking note is that of the brotherhood between the beginning and the end, the bond between life and death which should be kept taut in order

17. Quoted in *Sonetos espirituales,* ed. Ricardo Gullón (Madrid: Aguado, 1957), pp. 15, 17.
18. *Eighty Poems of Antonio Machado,* trans. Willis Barnstone (New York: Las Américas, 1959), p. 5.

to give meaning to existence. The following poem is a masterpiece of its kind:

¿Cómo, muerte, tenerte
miedo? ¿No estás aquí conmigo, trabajando?
¿No te toco en mis ojos; no me dices
que no sabes de nada, que eres hueca,
inconsciente y pacífica? ¿No gozas,
conmigo, todo: gloria, soledad,
amor, hasta tus tuétanos?
¿No me estás aguantando,
muerte, de pie, la vida?
¿No te traigo y te llevo, ciega,
como tu lazarillo? ¿No repites
con tu boca pasiva
lo que quiero que digas? ¿No soportas,
esclava, la bondad con que te obligo?
¿Qué verás, qué dirás, adónde irás
sin mí? ¿No seré yo,
muerte, tu muerte, a quien tú, muerte,
debes temer, mimar, amar?

(p. 655)

How can I fear you,
death? Do you not labor here, with me?
Do I not touch you in my eyes; do you not tell me
that you know nothing, are hollow,
unconscious, and peaceful? Do you not enjoy
everything, with me: glory, solitude,
love, unto the marrow of your bones?
Do you not endure life for me,
death, erectly?
Do I not bring and take you in your blindness
like a guide? Do you not repeat
with your passive mouth
what I wish you to say? Do you not support,
like a slave, the kindness with which I obligate you?
What could you see or say, where could you go
without me? Might not I,
death, be your death, whom you, O death,
should fear, indulge, and love?

In phrases that echo John Donne's characterization of death as
". . . slave to Fate, Chance, kings and desperate men," Jiménez

underlines the humanity of our destiny. By employing a series of rhetorical questions and attempting to banish fear through physical and affective identification, the Spanish poet translates death into man's terms and makes it dependent upon the individual. The vocabulary depicts humble human acts: what is more intimate than to labor side by side, or more ironic than to serve as blind death's *lazarillo?* (The word comes from the name of the small boy who guided a vicious blind beggar through the streets of Salamanca in *Lazarillo de Tormes,* 1554, the first picaresque novel.) The anguish that marks our confrontation with death, the stupid senselessness that many twentieth-century writers have felt, dissolve in the profound irony and serenity of this poem. Paradoxically, it was written by a man whose life was tortured by a pathological dread of his final hour.[19]

If life is an apprenticeship for death, sleep is part of the learning. Like Unamuno (who called sleep the apostle of death) and many other writers, Jiménez was especially aware that to sleep is to die a little. Unlike Unamuno, however, his reaction to this fact is tranquil:

> ¡Cómo aprendemos a morir
> en ti, sueño!
> ¡Con qué belleza majistral
> nos vas llevando—por jardines,
> que nos parecen cada vez más nuestros—
> al gran conocimiento de la sombra!
> (p. 647)

> How we learn to die
> in you, O sleep!
> With what masterly beauty
> you gradually guide us—through gardens
> that seem more and more our own—
> to the great knowledge of shadow!

19. For further analysis of the bond between life and death, see my article, "Two Poems on Death by Juan Ramón Jiménez," *Modern Language Notes,* LXXV (1960), 502–7. The paradox remains: Juan Ramón's was a literary triumph over death. A psychologist who saw him in Washington, during one of his periods of depression, noted that ". . . he was possessed by death."—Theodore Lidz, "Juan Ramón Jiménez—A Remembrance," *The Yale Review,* LI (1961), 342.

## Final Encounter

". . . and gather me
into the artifice of eternity."
Yeats, "Sailing to Byzantium"

The national violence produced by the Spanish Civil War—
that terrible war of three centuries, as Jiménez called it—
forced Juan Ramón and Zenobia to return to America. They
were warmly received, and Jiménez gave classes for a while at
the University of Maryland. As if pulled by a magnet, they
moved southward, and, after a stay in Coral Gables, Florida,
settled in Puerto Rico, where the sunshine and the language
could in part compensate for the lost Andalusia. Another sea
voyage, this time to Buenos Aires and Montevideo in 1948,
proved nearly as influential as the first one.

With his environment exploding in violence and the dis-
quieting experience of travel forced upon him again, Jiménez
turned to his final phase, or, as he baptized it, his "third road,"
notable for the successful conclusion of his siege of beauty and
the achievement of the unity he so faithfully sought. However,
as I hope to show, the great moment partook of a heightened
awareness of his human attributes. It was, in large measure, a
spiritual-humanistic experience, and must be viewed as such for
a proper understanding of Jiménez, who is a religious poet in
his devotion to an ideal and in his single-minded zeal, but who
does not respond to any narrow orthodox interpretation.

*The Total Season (La estación total),* comprising verse
written from 1923 to 1936, is another transitional book, if one
may ever properly use the phrase in a writer whose change is so
gradual as to be no more perceptible than a gently graded
mountain road which arrives, nevertheless, after a suitable in-
terval, at a breathtaking view. The following proclamation
represents the usual need to transcend, now reaching a new
stage:

Ya no sirve esta voz ni esta mirada.
No nos basta esta forma. Hay que salir

y ser en otro ser el otro ser.
Perpetuar nuestra esplosión gozosa.

(p. 768)

This voice nor this glance no longer serve.
This form is not enough. One must go forth
and be in another being the other being.
Perpetuate our joyful explosion.

The *centro,* Jiménez' object of pursuit discovered in "Golfo" (*Diario*), is elaborated in *The Total Season,* its effect is savored, and its insight extended:

### Su sitio fiel

Las nubes y los árboles se funden
y el sol les trasparenta su honda paz.
Tan grande es la armonía del abrazo,
que la quiere gozar también el mar,
el mar que está tan lejos, que se acerca,
que ya se oye latir, que huele ya.

El cerco universal se va apretando,
y ya en toda la hora azul no hay más
que la nube, que el árbol, que la ola,
síntesis de la gloria cenital.
El fin está en el centro. Y se ha sentado
aquí, su sitio fiel, la eternidad.

Para esto hemos venido. (Cae todo
lo otro, que era luz provisional.)
Y todos los destinos aquí salen,
aquí entran, aquí suben, aquí están.
Tiene el alma un descanso de caminos
que han llegado a su único final.

(p. 782)

### Its Exact Site

The clouds and trees are fused,
the sun shines through their deep peace.
So great is the harmony of the embrace
that the sea too wishes to enjoy it,
the sea so far away, approaching now,
now smelled, now pounding heard.

The universal circle grows tighter;
now in all the blue hour there is only
the cloud, and the tree, and the wave,
synthesis of glory at its zenith.
The end is in the center. And eternity
has settled here its exact site.

For this we have come. (All else
succumbs; it was provisional light.)
All destinies here come forth,
here enter, here ascend, here are.
The soul feels like a road
arriving at its unique goal.

The "total center" houses the chief themes of his work—love, poetry, woman, and death. Brought together they provide a new awareness of the world, and Jiménez is quick to use "awareness" (sometimes called "loving awareness") as a synonym for the "total center." All elements and ideas flow inward now into the receptacle of mind. The formula *poetry equals spirit* is about to be established, but before this can be done, the relation between the subjective self and the world must be explored once more.

### THE POET AND THE WORLD

"Let the two of us gaze at each other."
*Tercera antolojía poética*, p. 926

The return to America aroused in Jiménez a confusion of space, time, and existence. To observe this discomfiture, we must turn to a long prose poem called "Space" ("Espacio"). Therein takes place a struggle between the ego and the world, tending toward the assimilation of both in the center of totality, or the creative awareness just described. It is the final struggle before the triumphant metaphysical éclat of his last book.

For the writer in exile, the discontinuity between man and the world is considerably heightened. He observes reality through two lenses, one colored by the memory of life in his native land and the other prescribed by the ambient of his new *patria*. If he is introspective, he must certainly become more aware than ever of mankind's odd relationship with physical reality—the contingency of being in this certain time and place —and, accordingly, he grows especially appreciative of that fragile but decisive instrument with which he faces reality: the human mind. Primarily the artist has, of course, always been concerned with transcending the fragmentary, accidental nature of existence in order to establish some kind of ordered relation between the mind and the world. It might be thought that in the case of an artist like Jiménez, with strong mystic tendencies, the problem would be solved rapidly by flight into a spiritual reality. But although Jiménez forever sought such experiences, he very much wanted to keep one foot on earth; accordingly, he was not tempted to make the classical mystic denunciation of mundane matters. Instead, he tried to enrich the here and now of existence, to bring to his point in space and time an aroused and loving awareness. Only then, in accordance with his last definition of poetry, could he raise the personal to the universal.

In the second fragment of "Space," worthy of quotation in full, he undertakes this task. The poignancy of exile underlies a stream of associations in which New York's Morningside Heights blurs with Spain, and every facet of present reality is fused with the lost reality of the past, including lines from previous poems. The poet's mind becomes a spacious playground, and the personal is raised to the universal but without sacrifice of the human limits of here and now:

> "In order to remember why I have lived," I come to you, Hudson River of my sea. "Sweet as this light was my love ..." "Beneath Washington Bridge (the great bridge which is most like New York) flows the yellow field of my childhood." Childhood: I become again and am a child, lost, so large, in what is the largest. Unexpected legend: "Sweet as the light is love," and this New York is the same as Moguer, is the same as Seville and Madrid. I am prey to the wind on the corner of Broadway as on the corner of my street called Rascón; and the door where I live is open, with sun within. "Sweet as this sun was love." I met one so in-

stalled, smiled at him, and climbed once again to the provisional corner of my solitude and my silence, just the same
on the ninth floor with sun as on the ground floor of my
street and sky. "Sweet as this sun is love." Familiar windows
and paintings of Murillo looked at me. In the screen of
blueness, the universal sparrow sang, the sparrow and I sang
and spoke; and I heard it as woman's voice in the wind of
the world. What a corner for my fantasy to occur! The sun
burned the south of my corner, and in the stunted spot in
the mat my illusion sweetly grew, wanting to flee from
golden meanness. "Underneath Washington Bridge, the
bridge that knows New York best, flows the golden field
of my childhood..." Full, I went down to the street, the
wind opened my clothing and my heart; I saw good faces.
In the garden of St. John the Divine the green poplars were
of Madrid; I spoke Spanish to a cat and a dog; and the
children of the choir, eternal language, equal in paradise and
on the moon, were singing, with the bells of St. John, in
the ray of straight sun, vivid, where the sky floated, become
harmony of violet and gold; ideal iris which descended and
ascended, descended... "Sweet as this sun was love." I went
out along Amsterdam, there was the moon (Morningside);
the air was so pure! not cold, fresh, fresh; in it came the
life of evening spring, and the sun was in the moon, the
present sun, the sun which nevermore would leave my bones
alone, sun in the blood and the wind. And absent I entered
singing into the arbor of night, and the river going below
Washington Bridge, still with sun, towards my Spain by my
east, to my eastern May of Madrid; a sun now dead, but
alive, a sun present, but absent; an ember sun of vital scarlet; a vital scarlet sun in greenness; a sun vital in greenness
now black; a sun in blackness now moon; a sun in the
great scarlet moon; a sun of new glory, new in another east;
a sun of love and lovely work; a sun like love... "Sweet as
this sun was love!"

(pp. 864–66)

Movingly Jiménez affirms a simple but important fact: the
bearded ascetic Spaniard wandering the streets of New York is
the same vessel of awareness that wandered the streets of Spain.
This apparently obvious realization was, nevertheless, of profound consequence because it enabled Jiménez to proclaim the

human mind as a free arbiter of reality unbound by time and space. The sparrow's song is universal because of man's awareness of it. Presence and absence, time and space—the "accidental frontiers" (p. 873), as he called them—are fused in the light of the mind.

However, we must not conclude that there is no other reality for Jiménez except mind. In defining the equation *world = ego* as a key to Jiménez, the critic Guillermo Díaz-Plaja states, "The world exists . . . as a function of the poetic ego; without the latter, there would be no world."[20] It is certainly possible to advance this interpretation on the basis of many of Jiménez' own words. In the third fragment of "Space," for example, he said, "But if I am not here with my five senses, neither the sea nor the wind are wind and sea; wind and sea are not rejoicing if I do not see them, if I do not say their names and write of their pleasure" (p. 872).

But there are just as many lines in his work which affirm the contrary. As early as 1910 he had written, "...And I shall depart. And the birds will remain / singing . . ." (p. 212). No, Jiménez did not solve the old problem of whether or not reality exists outside our ken. What he did proclaim in the joyful poetry of his final years is that only the human mind—especially the poet's mind—can speak of the sea as rejoicing. Only man can realize and define beauty. In loving awareness, man measures the beauty of his world; that is the human attribute which makes him divine:

> Belleza que yo he visto,
> ¡no te borres ya nunca!
> Porque seas eterna,
> ¡yo quiero ser eterno!
>
> (p. 375)

> Beauty which I have seen,
> do not erase yourself ever!
> So that you may be eternal,
> I wish to be eternal!

20. *Juan Ramón Jiménez en su poesía* (Madrid: Aguilar, 1958), p. 40.

Heidegger said that the poet establishes reality; Jiménez would reply that he beautifies it.

The inadequacy of criticism which makes the existence of the world depend on Jiménez' mind—in effect, accusing him of solipsism—is nowhere better underlined than in the solemn and moving description of the poet and a hawthorn tree. With great dignity, man and plant face each other under a blazing sun, equal, Jiménez avows, in stature, depth, and dreams:

Del fondo de la vida

En el pedral, un sol sobre un espino, mío.
Y mirándolo ¿yo?
.   .   .   .   .   .   .   .   .

Déjame que lo mire yo, este espino (y lo oiga)
de gritante sol fúljido, fuego sofocante
silencioso,
que ha sacado del fondo de la tierra
ese ser natural (tronco, hoja, espina)
de seca condición aguda;
sin más anhelo ni cuidado
que su color, su olor, su forma; y su sustancia,
y su esencia (que es su vida y su conciencia).
Una espresión distinta, que en el sol
grita en silencio lo que yo oigo, oigo.

Déjame que lo mire y considere.
Porque yo he sacado, diverso
también, del fondo de la tierra,
my form, my color, my odor; and my substance,
y mi esencia (que es mi vida y mi conciencia)
carne y hueso (con ojos indudables)
sin más cuidado ni ansia
que una palabra iluminada,
que una palabra fuljidente,
que una palabra fogueante,
una espresión distinta, que en el sol está gritando
silenciosa;
que quizás algo o alguien oiga, oiga.

Y, hombre frente a espino, aquí estoy, con el sol
(que no sé de qué especie puedo ser,

si un sol desierto me traspasa)
un sol, un igual sol, sobre dos sueños.

Déjanos a los dos que nos miremos.

(pp. 925–26)

### From the Depths of Life

On stony ground, a sun above a hawthorn, mine.
And gazing at it, I?

.    .    .    .    .    .    .    .

Let me look at it, this hawthorn (and hear it)
of shouting brilliant sun, suffocating fire
of silence,
that has drawn from the depths of earth
a natural being (trunk, leaf, thorn)
of sharp, dry condition;
with no more desire nor care
than its color, its odor, its form; and its substance,
and its essence (which is its life and its consciousness).
A different expression that in the sun
silently shouts all that I hear and hear.

Let me look at it and consider.
Because I have drawn, also
diversely, from the depths of earth,
my form, my color, my odor; and my substance,
and my essence (which is my life and my consciousness)
flesh and bone (with clear eyes)
with no care nor anxiety
than an illuminated word,
than a gleaming word,
than a thunder-clear word,
a different expression that in the sun is shouting
silently;
that perchance something or someone may hear and hear.

Man before hawthorn, here I am, with the sun
(I know not what species I can be,
if a deserted sun pierces me)
a sun, an equal sun, above two dreams.

Let the two of us gaze at each other.

THE POET AND HIS GOD

The craving of man's mind for some absolute form of knowledge has inspired many of the chief episodes of his history. To speak of the development of religion would be gratuitous, although today one can still recognize in the protean scrutiny of the world to which our scientific age is dedicated the same impulsive need for transcendent knowledge that shaped the course of religion. Physicists plumb the nature of matter, seeking the ultimate structure of the universe. Social scientists, armed with their formidable jargon, struggle to know all there is to know about human society. Existentialists proclaim man himself as the absolute.

In former times, certain individuals, seeking absolute knowledge, transcended their earthly being through the phenomenon of mysticism. In the sublime arms of God, they learned all, and surrendered their identity for a moment. Today these experiences still occur, although in less ecstatic ways. The psychological basis of Santa Teresa's raptures is not completely divorced from the drive that keeps the scientist in his laboratory all night: both minds are absorbed in discovery, both personalities engaged in something beyond themselves. In our age, the pressure that impels the scientist has tremendously concrete applications that, for all practical purposes, have obtained the worshipful respect of society. The mysticism of the saints had no such concrete fruits, and today it is viewed, if not with suspicion, at least with disdain, as selfish and impractical. To hold such an outlook is short-sighted, for the mystic urge, the desire for absolute experience, is, in some measure, part of the human character and not merely an aberration of alienated personalities.

Spanish culture, deficient in the scientific spirit, has been enthusiastically hospitable to mysticism as a form of religious and artistic expression. The Golden Age produced one of Europe's purest lyric voices in St. John of the Cross; and El Greco, within the brown walls of Toledo, painted figures that writhe like flames leaping to heaven. Madariaga correctly observed that every Spanish writer, however fleetingly, succumbs to the mystic impulse (in the twentieth century, the dour Basque novelist Pío Baroja has been a notable exception). For Juan Ramón Jiménez, the urge was of extraordinary intensity from the beginning, and his poetry is like an ascending ray of light sweeping higher and wider to encompass the absolute.

The publication of *Animal of Depth (Animal de fondo)* in 1949 marks Jiménez' joyful acclamation of mysticism as the final end of poetry. The book, which appeared in a bilingual French and Spanish edition, is both a spiritual autobiography, recapitulating his career in terms of the need "to depart without reason" that he first perceived during the ocean voyage to meet his bride, and a fusion of his poetic ideals in a new sense of creative unity with the world.

Jiménez' mysticism is a link in the chain of light forged in the tradition of St. John of the Cross but completely free of its attendant dogma. The poet's own notes support the unorthodoxy of his position: "Not that I write the usual kind of religious poetry; however, I consider poetry to be profoundly religious, that immanent religion without any creed whatsoever that I have always professed" (p. 1016). In even clearer accents, the first poem describes the god of this new volume:

> No eres mi redentor, ni eres mi ejemplo,
> ni mi padre, ni mi hijo, ni mi hermano;
> eres igual y uno, eres distinto y todo;
> eres dios de lo hermoso conseguido,
> conciencia mía de lo hermoso.
>
> (p. 963)

> You are not my redeemer, nor my example,
> nor my father, nor my son, nor my brother;
> you are equal and one, you are different and all;
> you are the god of attained beauty,
> my consciousness of what is beauty.

*Animal of Depth* is a hymn in celebration of the creative capabilities of the human mind, the total center, the loving awareness which perceives and names beauty. In the notes we read, ". . . beauty is within us and also at the same time without" (p. 1017); it constantly presses for the recognition that only man can give it. In a final metaphor, the human mind becomes a god "desired and desiring," wanted by the world and in turn desiring the world for the beauty it contains. The mind and its highly developed awareness equal a state of divinity, and the entire purpose of Jiménez' long career is revealed as an effort to carry the mind forward to divine awareness.

It may be seen, therefore, that *Animal of Depth* contains no abrupt break with the past. What is new is the shout of joy, the exultation that tugs at the reader. At the pinnacle of his years, Jiménez saw the labor of a lifetime finally resolved, and wrote his first book in which there is not a trace of despondency nor a touch of shadow. From the first word "transparency" to the last word "air," everything is bathed in light:

#### Todas las nubes arden

Todas las nubes arden
porque yo te he encontrado,
dios deseante y deseado;
antorchas altas cárdenas
(granas, azules, rojas, amarillas)
en alto grito de rumor de luz.

. . . . . . . .

Todas las nubes que existieron,
que existen y que existirán,
me rodean con signos de evidencia;
ellas son para mí
la afirmación alzada de este hondo
fondo de aire en que yo vivo;
el subir verdadero del subir,
el subir del hallazgo en lo alto profundo.

(pp. 971–72)

#### All the Clouds Ablaze

All the clouds blaze
because I have found you,
god desiring and desired;
high torches livid
(scarlet, blue, red, yellow)
in an elevated cry of latent light.

. . . . . . . .

> All the clouds that were,
> that are and shall be,
> surround me with signs of evidence;
> they are for me
> the lofty affirmation of this deep
> depth of air in which I live;
> the true ascension of ascent,
> the ascension of discovery in high profundity.

The devoted reader of Jiménez' prolonged poetic act is deeply moved to see all the familiar elements flowing into the arms of this lyric, creative god of light and awareness. It is as if the previous stages had been merely a rehearsal for this final great rôle. The fluctuation of the impressionist now appears as the reciprocity of awareness and attainment—"god desired and desiring." It becomes part of the rhythm of many poems, re-creating the motion of the waves. The sea once again serves as a total metaphor: "Here you form yourself in permanent / movement of lights and colors . . ." (p. 967). The former image of the mind lends itself naturally as a metaphor for the mind's divine wakefulness.

The light described in early poems as a golden haze of autumn reaches the intensity of a flame consuming mind and man together. Light is the traditional mystic agent of identification with the absolute:

> Dios del venir, te siento entre mis manos,
> aquí estás enredado conmigo, en lucha hermosa
> de amor, lo mismo
> que un fuego con su aire.
>
> (p. 963)

> God of arrival, I feel you in my hands,
> here you are entwined with me in a beautiful struggle
> of love, the same
> as fire with its air.

The "exact name of things" has, of course, been discovered:

> Yo he acumulado mi esperanza
> en lengua, en nombre hablado, en nombre escrito;
> a todo yo le había puesto nombre

y tú has tomado el puesto
de toda esta nombradía.

(p. 965)

I have gathered up my hope
in words, in the spoken name, the written name;
to everything I gave a name
and you have assumed the dignity
of every name.

Love, that greatest intuition of man's transcendental possibilities, has been a secure guide from the first days when it consisted of nothing more than response to the flesh of woman:

Tú eras, viniste siendo, eres el amor
en fuego, agua, tierra y aire,
amor en cuerpo mío de hombre y en cuerpo de mujer,
el amor que es la forma
total y única
del elemento natural, que es elemento
del todo, el para siempre; . . .

(p. 969)

You were, continued being, and are love
in fire, water, earth, and air,
love in this man-body of mine and in the body of woman,
love that is the form,
total and unique,
of the natural element, that is the element
of everything, eternity; . . .

These and other themes are acclaimed in the union of fire and air that forges the divine poetic task. With reason could he cry in elation, ". . . now I have my totality . . ." (p. 1005).

Clarification of Jiménez' precise relation to Western mysticism would be a lengthy task. However, we may look briefly at his relation to St. John of the Cross, a mystic poet of the same tradition, in order to read the late poems with increased understanding. St. John, for example, emphasized the complete surrender of intelligence during the mystic seizure: "One of the greatest favors bestowed on the soul transiently in this life is to enable it to see so distinctly and feel so profoundly that it cannot comprehend

God at all."[21] Juan Ramón in his mystical experiences never abandoned the need to comprehend. Radically aware of the gulf between himself and the absolute, he labored to fill it, and even as he succeeded, maintained a kind of detachment. His body, he says in one poem, encircles, that is, comprehends, the divinity of his consiousness. St. John selected a total metaphor—that of human love—and described his rapture in these terms. Jiménez moves in and out of a series of metaphors—earth, air, fire, body—constantly exploring the facets of his "beautiful struggle" with the god who is both desired and desiring.

In the matter of language, Jiménez' courtship of the ineffable is more intellectual than St. John's. Whereas the latter believed that through figurative language—the symbols of poetry—one could only approximate a description of the mystic state, Juan Ramón regarded the creation of this language as a mystical act in itself, subject to guidance and scrutiny by the intellect. His overriding concern with words (displayed until the end by the neologisms abounding in *Animal of Depth*), the large number of poems about poetry, the often fussy but always persistent preoccupation with himself creating—these characteristics betray the artificer of words, the intellectual who could not always give himself unquestioningly to language as did St. John of the Cross.

With regard to dogma, Jiménez' brand of mysticism has many categorical differences from the traditional Catholic type. In fact, *Animal of Depth* is a book notable for the absence of Catholic inspiration. As Concha Zardoya pointed out, the soul has not become bare; instead, it has been enriched.[22] It has not been cleansed but rather amplified ("I have nothing to purge" [p. 963]). There is no ascetic denial of oneself, rather the fullest acceptance. Therefore, despite the customary vocabulary of Spanish mysticism (fire, flame, torch, grace, ascension, sun),

21. Trans. by J. B. Trend and quoted by Aldous Huxley, *The Perennial Philosophy* (London: Chatto & Windus, 1946), p. 33.
22. "El dios deseado y deseante de *Animal de fondo*," *Insula,* XII, Nos. 128–29 (1957), p. 20.

*Animal of Depth,* if rightly read, accords only accidentally with that tradition.

Rudolph Otto, in his comparative analysis of the nature of mysticism, delineates two general types of mystic experience: one is inward, the other outward. Sánchez Barbudo places Juan Ramón in the latter camp, and it is here that we can best comprehend the cycle of poems comprising *Animal of Depth.*[23] Jiménez' desire for unification is with the world around him; his soul, the divine awareness that he possesses, moves toward an object such as a tree, a hill, or the sky, and joins with it, causing both to be born again in an ideal world. During this experience, our traditional notions of dualities of mind and matter or body and soul must be abandoned. Then we may realize, as Whitehead said, that "There is no real dualism between eternal lakes and hills, on the one hand, and personal feelings, on the other. . . ."[24] Explaining his last book, Jiménez wrote, ". . . the goal of my vocation . . . was this superior . . . state of awareness . . ." (p. 1018).

One would expect all antitheses to be resolved in the divine center of awareness. And so they are—root, wing; land, sky; light, shadow; alien, personal; beginning, end: all reach an agreement. Now the paradox expressed in the *Diary*— "Roots and wings. But let the wings / take root and the roots fly" (p. 18)—seems less contradictory, especially if we construe root to equal body and wing to equal soul and if, furthermore, we realize that Jiménez desired the transcendence of man's total nature, which would mean his physical as well as spiritual endowments. In *Animal of Depth,* he coined a new word—*cuerpialma,* bodysoul—to describe the intimacy between matter and spirit, or, as he called it, the encounter of reality and its image. Precisely because he refused to discard the root element of the body, he can never be accepted as an orthodox religious mystic. The flesh sheltering his spirit is fully recognized:

23. *La segunda época de Juan Ramón Jiménez (1916–1953)* (Madrid: Gredos, 1962), pp. 196–98.

24. *Science and the Modern World,* quoted in Edmund Wilson, *Axel's Castle* (New York: Scribner's, 1940), p. 5.

Esta conciencia que me rodeó
en toda mi vivida,
como halo, aura, atmósfera de mi ser mío,
se me ha metido ahora dentro.

Ahora el halo es de dentro
y ahora es mi cuerpo centro
visible de mí mismo; soy, visible,
cuerpo maduro de este halo,
lo mismo que la fruta, que fue flor
de ella misma, es ahora la fruta de mi flor.

.   .   .   .   .   .   .   .

Dios, ya soy la envoltura de mi centro,
de ti dentro.

(pp. 973–74)

This awareness that encircled me
in all my living,
a halo, aura, atmosphere of my own being,
has entered now within me.

The halo is now within,
my body now the visible
center of myself; visible, I am
the ripe body of this halo,
just as fruit that was first
its own flower is now the fruit of my flower.

.   .   .   .   .   .   .   .

God, I am the sheath of my center,
of you within.

Jiménez' notion of beauty (which was all he could know of spirit) was inextricably bound to the here and now of the body and its senses. To the four primitive philosophical elements of fire, water, air, and earth, he added a fifth: human flesh. Those who cannot or will not accept this, misread him in one of two ways: either as a Catholic poet *manqué*, or as an aesthetic recluse, eccentrically protecting himself from human reality as much as possible. No more poignant presentation of the tragic human dichotomy has been made than in the third fragment of "Space," given its final editing in 1954:

With great difficulty can flesh have loved its soul more than my body loved you . . . because you were for it the ideal sum, and it became through you, with you, what it is.... Tell me again: Do you not weep to leave me? Why must you leave me, spirit? Did you not like my life? I sought your essence. What substance can the gods give your essence that I could not give you? I have already told you: "The gods had no more substance than I."

(pp. 1014–15)

When Yeats said that "An aged man is but a paltry thing, / . . . unless / Soul clap its hands and . . . louder sing," he was assuming the traditional position of Western asceticism. Jiménez, in his challenge to the soul to find a better house than the body—*his* body—is raising a unique cry, one that stamps his entire work.

The import of the title can now be appreciated—*Animal of Depth,* that is, a human being of earth and dust but containing also a deep well of light:

> Pero tú, dios, también estás en este fondo
> y a esta luz ves, venida de otro astro;
> tú estás y eres
> lo grande y lo pequeño que yo soy,
> en una proporción que es ésta mía,
> infinita hacia un fondo
> que es el pozo sagrado de mí mismo.
>
> .    .    .    .    .    .    .    .    .    .    .
>
> soy animal de fondo de aire
> con alas que no vuelan en al aire,
> que vuelan en la luz de la conciencia
> mayor que todo el sueño
> de eternidades e infinitos
> que están después, sin más que ahora yo, del aire.

(pp. 1014–15)

> But you, god, are also in this depth
> and, by this light come from another star, you see;
> you are
> the greatness and smallness that I am,
> in a proportion that is mine alone,
> infinite towards a deepness
> that is the sacred well of myself.

. . . . . . . . . .

I am an animal of the depth of air
with wings that do not fly in the air,
that fly in the light of awareness,
greater than the entire dream
of eternities and infinities
which are afterwards, with no more than I now, of the air.

SELECTED WORKS
OF JUAN RAMÓN JIMÉNEZ
(*In order of publication*)

### Poetry

*Arias tristes.* Madrid: Fernando Fe, 1903.

*Pastorales* (*1903–1905*). Madrid: Renacimiento, 1911.

*Sonetos espirituales* (*1914–1915*). Madrid: Calleja, 1917.

*Diario de un poeta recién casado* (*1916*). Madrid: Calleja, 1917; title changed to *Diario de poeta y mar* (Buenos Aires: Losada, 1948; Madrid: Aguado, 1955).

*Eternidades* (*1916–1917*). Madrid: Calleja, 1918.

*Piedra y cielo* (1917–1918). Madrid: Fortanet, 1919.

*Segunda antolojía poética* (1898–1918). Madrid: Impr. Clásica Española, 1920; Madrid: Espasa-Calpe, 1955. A "re-created" selection of previous work made by the author.

*Belleza* (*en verso*) (*1917–1923*). Madrid: J. R. Jiménez y Z. C. de Jiménez, 1923.

*Poesía* (*en verso*) (*1917–1923*). Madrid: J. R. Jiménez y Z. C. de Jiménez, 1923; Buenos Aires: Losada, 1946.

*"La estación total" con las "Canciones de la nueva luz."* Buenos Aires: Losada, 1946.

*Animal de fondo.* Buenos Aires: Pleamar, 1949.

*Tercera antolojía poética* (*1898–1953*). Madrid: Biblioteca Nueva, 1957. A final selection of his work, made in collaboration with his wife, and, in the case of *Poesía* and *Belleza,* Eugenio Florit.

### Prose

*Platero y yo, elegía andaluza.* Madrid: La Lectura, 1914. There is a very popular English translation by Eloïse Roach (Austin: University of Texas Press, 1957), as well as one by William and Mary Roberts (Oxford: Dolphin, 1956).

*Españoles de tres mundos: Viejo mundo. Nuevo mundo. Otro mundo* (*Caricatura lírica*) (*1914–1940*). Buenos Aires: Losada, 1944. A new, enlarged edition under the care of Ricardo Gullón, who contributes a penetrating essay on the art of the literary portrait in Jiménez, was published in 1960 by Aguado in Madrid.

## ENGLISH
### TRANSLATIONS

After Jiménez received the Nobel Prize in 1956, English translations began to appear. Eloïse Roach's version of *Platero y yo*, mentioned above, attained the dubious fame of a "spread" in *Life* and *Time*. H. R. Hays, as the translator of *The Selected Writings of Juan Ramón Jiménez* (New York: Farrar, Straus, and Cudahy, 1957), occasionally displays a lack of ear and a tendency towards inaccuracies. The selection is thoroughly representative, however, and the preface by Eugenio Florit, one of Juan Ramón's confidants and a perceptive poet in his own right, provides an informative introduction. The work obviously suffers from the demand for quick publicity imposed by the Nobel Prize. Facing Spanish originals are lacking.

Previous to the stir caused by the Nobel award, the English Hispanist J. B. Trend published *Fifty Spanish Poems* (New York: Oxford University Press, 1950; Berkeley: University of California Press, 1951), highly controversial translations in which many liberties are taken in an attempt to re-create the subtle grace of Jiménez' Spanish. The results are dubious. Eleanor L. Turnbull, with her usual old-fashioned tone, has various translations in *Ten Centuries of Spanish Poetry* (Baltimore, Md.: Johns Hopkins Press, 1955), pp. 426–47.

In my opinion, the most successful translations have been by W. S. Merwin, Rachel Frank, and Julia Howe in *Poetry*, LXXXIII (1953), 184–224, and by Carlos de Francisco Zea in *The Fifties*, No. 2 (1959), pp. 24–33. *The Poem Itself*, ed. Stanley Burnshaw (New York: Holt, 1960), pp. 182–89, contains four literal translations and commentary by Eugenio Florit. One may consult J. M. Cohen's "plain prose" translations in *The Penguin Book of Spanish Verse* (London: Penguin Books, 1960), pp. 351–59. The brief descriptive sketch concerning Juan Ramón (p. xxii) is an example of how poets may be distorted by anthologists.

The selection in *An Anthology of Spanish Poetry* (New York: Anchor, 1961), pp. 273–86, is too brief but contains some good translating by Lysander Kemp, Willis Barnstone and Kate Flores.

One of Juan Ramón's most devoted translators has been Eloïse Roach, whose version of *Platero y yo* was so well received in 1957. In *Three Hundred Poems, 1903–1953* (Austin: University of Texas

Press, 1962), she has made a personal selection of fifty years of Jiménez' poetry. Miss Roach has her admirers. She is certainly sensitive to the poet's purpose, and her eye for flowers and color is as delicate as his. But often her translations explain too much, and there are occasions for quarreling with meaning. Why, to cite only one of many examples, should *noble paz* become "grateful peace" (p. 72)?

# IV

# Federico García Lorca

---

## The Magic of Reality

. . . the dark root of the cry.
*Blood Wedding,* III, iii

# Rhyme and Personality

The fame of Federico García Lorca, already considerable while he was still alive, spread rapidly throughout the civilized world as a result of his execution by a Fascist firing squad in 1936. The circumstances of his tragic end made him a hero among left-wing intellectuals of the thirties and shocked sensitive people of all persuasions. Lorca the man, as always, remained inseparable from Lorca the poet. Those, however, who peevishly doubted his real worth, fearing it had been exaggerated by a political accident, were wrong. Lorca's fame has continued to increase. His poetry alone has been translated into nine languages, including fifteen versions in French and more than that number in English.

During a moment when Western verse is beginning to shrug off the intellectual mantle of T. S. Eliot and Paul Valéry, the immediacy and emotional shock of Lorca's poetry takes on special importance. Lorca is exciting and disturbing in a way that no intellectual poet can be. The parallel to Dylan Thomas comes at once to mind and is very apt. Both men were unable to separate their poetry from their lives, both stimulated a legend while still alive, and both brought to the reading of their own verse a special power that unsettled and aroused their listeners.

Lorca's personality gave the impression of a man for whom song was the equivalent of life and silence the ultimate terror. Possessing overwhelming vitality, spirited imagination, a disconcerting smile, and no mean musical ability, he charmed everyone he met by his intense ingenuity and his gift of turning all that he touched into poetry. Like a child, he was in a state of constant delight with the world. A friend recalls being roused late one night by a knock on the door which turned out to be Lorca, bubbling with excitement from having seen a shoe hanging from a tree. "It's tremendous," Lorca had urged, "you must come and see it."[1] Such a state of natural wonder had its counterpart in fits of dark depression. "Those who thought of him as a gaily colored bird did not know him," wrote the poet Vicente Aleixandre.[2] A deep elemental sadness, a fear akin to wonder, often took hold of him, and accounts for the strange mixture of terror and beauty in his work.

The fusion of poetry and personality explains his notorious reluctance to publish. It did not occur to him that his vitality should be locked into a printing press and distributed by means of symbols throughout the world. Instead he read his poetry at small gatherings and sent autograph copies to his friends, who constantly had to badger him into committing his verse to publication. Hence his reputation, in keeping with the minstrel quality of his career, first flourished independently of the printed word.

Lorca's temperment also embodied the vital urge toward self-expression that is typical of the Spanish people, particularly those of Andalusia, where he was born about a dozen miles from Granada in 1898. The folk culture of Andalusia revolves around the "deep song" or *cante jondo,* a naked lament raised against the indifference of the world. It was in these songs that Lorca first felt the dark roots of art that dominate most of his poetry. He became the troubadour of Andalusia and elevated its folklore to the level of sophisticated poetry. He was so success-

1. Carlos Morla Lynch, *En España con Federico García Lorca* (Madrid: Aguilar, 1957), p. 27.
2. "Federico," Epilogue to Federico García Lorca, *Obras completas* (Madrid: Aguilar, 1960), p. 1789. Lorca's poetry and prose are quoted from this edition. Lorca's works are copyright by the Estate of Federico García Lorca. Reprinted by permission of the Estate of Federico García Lorca and New Directions, Publishers.

fully associated with this region of Spain that eventually he felt limited by it. Perusal of his letters reveals how ambivalent his attitude was towards the main source of his inspiration.

Arriving in Madrid in the spring of 1919, he entered the Residencia de Estudiantes on the Calle del Pinar and began to make his whimsical way in the artistic world of the capital. The Residencia was an intellectual center of high ideals, the heir of the Institución Libre de Enseñanza that had formed Antonio Machado's generation, and it was open to influence from all quarters. For Lorca it offered valuable contact with other writers and artists, some of them, like Salvador Dalí, busy outraging the bourgeoisie.

Critics are fond of pointing out that Lorca was not an intellectual. They remind us that he had been a distracted student at the University of Granada, having failed in literature, and that he read fewer books than any of his contemporaries. Most of what he knew about the literary currents of his time, he absorbed from the conversation of other writers.[3] Although this point has been over-emphasized, it does appear to be true that Lorca was a natural poet, whose light and enchanted spirit would have been made sluggish by a heavy diet of reading. Fortunately, the viable Spanish tradition of popular, non-academic art allowed Lorca to be accepted readily by the Madrid literati. Nevertheless, his letters disclose that he smarted occasionally from feelings of inferiority: "I am not intelligent, it's true! But I am a poet." In a pathetic but also waggish letter to Jorge Guillén, he declared his intention of becoming a professor of literature in order to gain the respect of his family (which was opposed to his writing poetry without "planning anything"), and asked how to go about it. Guillén advised him to buy a filing cabinet and begin taking notes, knowing, perhaps unconsciously, that nothing was more foreign to Lorca's nature. The latter replied half-defensively that since he always noticed

3. Angel del Río, *Vida y obras de Federico García Lorca* (Saragossa: Heraldo de Aragón, 1952), p. 18.

strange things about authors, the notes he took would be not-able indeed.[4] The filing cabinet was never purchased.

Lorca did read poets with whom he felt an affinity, and his lecture on Góngora in 1927 is not only "intelligent," it also maps the technique of modern metaphor. He was not, however, a poet of "ideas," and there is no "message" in his work except an appeal for spontaneity. Yet the total effect of his verse, the impact of his letters and lectures, reveal a serious, conscientious, devoted, and self-aware artist, who was in command of himself and who used his intelligence to control, without diminishing, the wildness of his emotions.

The success of the *Gypsy Ballad-Book* (*Romancero gitano*) in 1928 startled and dismayed him. He had written to Guillén that when he finished this book he would never touch the gypsy theme again. "I do not wish to be pigeonholed," he cried, "nor considered merely a 'savage poet'" (p. 1580). The nagging defensiveness about intellectuality remained. Further impelled by a personal crisis, he decided to seek a change of atmosphere, and, at the suggestion of Fernando de los Ríos, chose to go to New York instead of the usual haven of Paris.

He arrived in the summer of 1929. It was his first visit to a foreign country, and New York's steel jungle thoroughly over-whelmed him. Professor del Río, his friend at Columbia Uni-versity, remembers Lorca walking the streets and exclaiming in a mixture of humor and terror, "I don't understand a thing!" To aggravate his feelings came the economic collapse in the fall of '29. *Poet in New York,* published posthumously in 1940, was the result of this experience. Born of a triple crisis—per-sonal, literary, and social—it is a book that critics have only re-cently begun to evaluate properly.[5] Like the city in which it was written, *Poet in New York* overpowers the casual visitor, re-serving its raw wonders for the less transient.

He finally fled to Cuba in the spring of 1930, and happiness

4. Letters written to Jorge Guillén in 1927, *Obras,* pp. 1575, 1584. See also Guillén, *Federico en persona* (Buenos Aires: Emecé, 1959), p. 95.
5. Angel del Río, *Poeta en Nueva York* (Madrid: Taurus, 1958), pp. 9–20.

returned. Just as Juan Ramón and Zenobia suddenly found themselves at home in Puerto Rico, Lorca too responded to the transplanted version of southern Spain in the Caribbean, warming himself in the sun and feeling the intense frustration of New York evaporate in the gentle climate of the island that Christopher Columbus had compared to Andalusia in April. For some time he had been struggling to cast off what he considered to be the provincial tradition of Andalusia. After New York, he recognized it instead as the source of his strength and, consciously or unconsciously, decided to work within it and cease worrying about intellectual poetry. His intuition was right. The brilliant elegy he wrote in 1934 on the death of the bullfighter Ignacio Sánchez Mejías could not be more Andalusian, more Spanish, and more universal as it moves from agony to peaceful acceptance. Like Yeats, Lorca owed his pure lyric voice to a strong native tradition, one that both men had the sense and ability to exploit in their own terms.

Feverish and fruitful activity followed his return to Spain in the summer of 1930. He began to cultivate the pronounced dramatic element in his poetry and to write some of the most successful verse drama of the century.[6] *Blood Wedding* (1933) and *Yerma* (1934) combine lyricism and prose (a prose so lyric it can hardly hold its shape) in the projection of the theme of sexual violence and frustration against the backdrop of Andalusia. In *The House of Bernarda Alba,* presented posthumously in Buenos Aires in 1945, he proved that his prose was capable of both simplicity and tragic intensity.

During the idealistic and unstable days of the Spanish Republic, he organized a traveling theater, "La Barraca," in order to carry classical Spanish plays to small towns. In this, as in much else, his likeness to the seventeenth-century playwright Lope de Vega is notable.

The amount of poetry he wrote diminished as his theatrical

---

6. Lorca's plays are ". . . theatre-poetry which lives naturally on the modern stage."—Francis Fergusson, *The Human Image in Dramatic Literature* (New York: Anchor, 1957), p. 85.

efforts increased. Aside from the elegy to his bullfighter friend, there is no great poem for this period. He was experimenting with loose imitations of Arabic lyric forms, the results of which were published posthumously in 1940 as *Divan at the Tamarit,* and he has left "The Sonnets of Dark Love," evidently the beginning of a series of poems which reflect, within the strictures of rigid technical control, a deep abiding unrest.

The great are often not permitted to die humbly. In Lorca's case it was as if the violence that haunts so many of his pages suddenly became malignant and struck him down. Legend, having enwrapped his life, now also conceals the details of his death. Although the immediate events connected with his assassination have been partially clarified by Gerald Brenan,[7] political propaganda and personal reticence still shroud the actual reason for the brutal deed. Lorca was not shot on account of his political persuasions because apparently he never had any. He did, however, have many political friends—both on the Right and the Left, including a Socialist brother-in-law who was the mayor of Granada—so that political reasons may have provided an excuse for his death. But the ultimate reason appears to have been that Lorca's libertine conduct and disdain for social mores had scandalized the ultraconservative members of Spanish society, and during the wave of anarchy that swept Spain after Franco's revolt on July 17, 1936, someone saw the chance to dispose of an "undesirable." Thus Lorca joined the ranks of those unhappy victims of the malign resentment that festers just below the surface of Spanish society and that suddenly spread like a fever in 1936, claiming Reds and Fascists, priests and atheists, in a kind of national vendetta. That he became a political hero of the Left is understandable but ironic.

In that fateful summer of 1936, he had to postpone plans for a return visit to America to supervise the production of his plays. As the violence mounted, he decided that Granada might be safer than Madrid. The return to Andalusia was symbolic and final. He was denounced, taken by armed car to a Falangist

7. *The Face of Spain* (New York: Grove Press, 1956), pp. 131–60.

camp in the hills of Víznar outside the city, and shot at dawn in a nearby ravine.

To one familiar with Lorca's poems and letters, the image of the poet in front of rifle barrels is unbearable. The responsibility is Spain's alone and peculiar to her atmosphere, but one sees in it a glimpse of the even greater outrages that were about to occur elsewhere in Europe. Lorca's death was the prelude to an era of violence.

The fearful silence finally came, and the epitaphs abound. The dominant picture is the poet possessed by the muse, the bard whirling to the sacred dance:

> for he on honey-dew hath fed,
> and drunk the milk of Paradise.

# The Language of Flowers and Stones

A childhood spent playing in meadows and gazing at crumpled violet mountains—such is the background recollected by Lorca himself (p. 99) for his first book, called simply *Book of Poems* (*Libro de poemas*, 1921). It provides a remarkable glimpse of a career in embryo, and its lapses are redeemed by much charming candor. Aside from touches of Jiménez and Machado, and a faint note of Verlaine, Lorca's talent is already independent, glowing with impudence, daring, and wit.

The sparkle of Lorca's style sets him off sharply from the ruminative aestheticism of Juan Ramón Jiménez and the lingering melancholy of Antonio Machado. Whereas Machado was content to probe again and again into the connotations of a few words, Lorca eagerly experimented with new arrangements. Jiménez felt at certain times in his career that the best poem was one without words, but Lorca was enchanted with language. The possibilities of metaphor appeared endless to him. He was like a magician anxious to transform reality through the sorcery of words. At this early stage in his development, the prime ingredients of his magic were humor, irony, and whimsy:

Paisaje

Las estrellas apagadas
llenan de ceniza el río
verdoso y frío.

La fuente no tiene trenzas.
Ya se han quemado los nidos
escondidos.

Las ranas hacen del cauce
una siringa encantada,
desafinada.

Sale del monte la luna,
con su cara bonachona
de jamona.

Una estrella le hace burla
desde su casa de añil
infantil.

El débil color rosado
hace cursi el horizonte
del monte.

Y observo que el laurel tiene
cansancio de ser poético
y profético.

. . . . . . . . . .

Un murciélago me avisa
que el sol se esconde doliente
en el poniente.

. . . . . . . . . .

En el carbón de la tarde
miro mis ojos lejanos,
cual milanos.

. . . . . . . . . .

Ya es de noche y las estrellas
clavan puñales al río
verdoso y frío.

(pp. 153-55)

Landscape
The slaked stars
fill with ashes the river
greenish cold.

The fountain has no tresses.
Hidden nests have all
been burned.

Frogs turn the river bed
into an enchanted flute,
slightly out of tune.

From behind the mountain appears the moon
with the kind, plump face
of a lady no longer young.

A star makes fun of her
from its childish house
of indigo.

The weak pink color
is in bad taste on the mountain's
horizon.

I notice that the laurel tree
is weary of being poetic
and prophetic.

.      .      .      .      .      .      .

A bat warns me
that the aching sun has hidden
in the west.

.      .      .      .      .      .      .

In the coal-black afternoon
I gaze at my distant eyes,
like kite birds.

.      .      .      .      .      .      .

Night has come and the stars
sink their knives into the river
greenish cold.

The imagery has a logical clarity typical of Lorca's metaphor. "Slaked stars" suggest "ashes," and "tresses" provide "nests." This marriage between reality and fantasy will be sustained. What is lacking is inspiration, or *duende,* Lorca's name for the dark spirit behind all art. Instead, the poem is an exercise in imagery. His creative skill was awaiting the impetus of the *cante jondo.*

Sadness in these early poems has the air of being borrowed

from the turn of the century, and lacks verisimilitude. He recognized but could not properly express the vein of despair that was part of his nature:

> la oculta pedrería
> de tristeza inconsciente que reluce
> al fondo de mi vida.
>
> (p. 207)
>
> the hidden jewelry
> of unconscious sadness glimmering
> in the depths of my life.

Light gaiety and conversations with flowers and stones charm these youthful pages. Snatches of popular songs flit through them, and a playfulness rooted in childish thought finds expression in the little things of nature:

> El lagarto viejo
>
> En la agostada senda
> he visto al buen lagarto
> (gota de cocodrilo)
> meditando.
> Con su verde levita
> de abate del diablo,
> su talante correcto
> y su cuello planchado,
> tiene un aire muy triste
> de viejo catedrático.
>
> .     .     .     .     .
>
> ¿Qué buscáis en la senda,
> filósofo cegato...?
>
> .     .     .     .     .
>
> ¡Volved a vuestra casa
> bajo el pueblo de grillos!
> (pp. 174–76)
>
> The Old Lizard
>
> Along the parched path
> I have seen the good lizard
> (a dash of crocodile)
> meditating.

> With his green frock coat
> like the devil's abbé,
> his countenance correct
> and collar pressed,
> he has the sad air
> of an old professor.
>
> .        .        .        .        .        .
>
> What do you seek along the path,
> nearsighted philosopher...?
>
> .        .        .        .        .        .
>
> Go back to your house
> under the crickets' village!

Tentatively present in his first book are two major themes that lead us into Lorca's intuitive outlook upon life and art. They are expressed in the opposing concepts of sight versus sightlessness and song versus silence.

For Lorca, the act of looking is immensely vital, symbolizing life itself. In his lecture on Góngora, he rated sight as the first of the five senses (p. 70), and his images are predominantly visual and then tactile. Thus, looks and glances in *Book of Poems* produce concrete effects. They scratch (p. 130), wound (p. 150), or draw webs like spiders (p. 154). *Sin ojos* (without eyes) is a fearful state, the loss of contact with reality, and therefore death. The imagery developed from these opposite poles acquires full pathetic force in ensuing books.[8]

Song and silence display a similar relationship. The cicada, or locust, with its shrill, noisy sound in late summer, is a symbol for song:

> ¡Cigarra!
>
> ¡Cigarra!
> ¡Dichosa tú!,

---

8. Sightlessness is also related to the image of facelessness in *Poet in New York*. Richard Saez compares the ". . . striking similarity between T. S. Eliot's use of eyes as a symbol of fertility or salvation . . . in *The Waste Land* and *The Hollow Men* and the frequent appearance of eyes in *Poet in New York*." See "The Ritual Sacrifice in Lorca's *Poet in New York*," in Manuel Durán, ed., *Lorca: A Collection of Critical Essays* (New Haven: Yale University Press, 1962), p. 110.

que sobre el lecho de tierra
mueres borracha de luz.

Tú sabes de las campiñas
el secreto de la vida,
y el cuento de hada vieja
que nacer la hierba sentía
en ti quedóse guardado.

.    .    .    .    .    .

Todo lo vivo que pasa
por las puertas de la muerte
va con la cabeza baja
y un aire blanco durmiente.
Con habla de pensamiento.
Sin sonidos...
Tristemente,
cubierto con el silencio
que es el manto de la muerte.

Mas tú, cigarra encantada,
derramando son, te mueres
y quedas transfigurada
en sonido y luz celeste.

.    .    .    .    .    .

Sea mi corazón cigarra
sobre los campos divinos.

(pp. 116–17)

Cicada!

Cicada!
Fortunate creature,
upon the lap of earth
you die drunk with light!

You know the fields'
secret of life;
in you is hidden
the tale of the ancient fairy
who heard the grass growing.

.    .    .    .    .    .

All living things that pass
through the doors of death
go with a lowered head

and a sleepy white air.
With the speech of thought.
Without sound...
Sadly,
covered with silence,
the mantle of death.

But you, enchanted cicada,
spilling sound, upon your death
are transfigured
into noise and celestial light.

.     .     .     .     .     .

Let my heart be a cicada
above the blessed fields.

Silence, like blindness, equals death, and speech or song is
equivalent to light, and, thereby, to sight. The impulse to sing
was vital to Lorca; the state of inexpressiveness preposterous.
Sound soon became transformed into the shout (*grito*) of the
*cante jondo,* and in *Poet in New York,* it reappears metamor-
phosed in the theme of the child struggling to be born.

In the metaphor of the silent dead bowed down with the
speech of thought, Lorca betrayed his feelings about intellec-
tualization and analysis. Naturally intuitive in his relations toward art and life, he refrained from muffling his music with a
great deal of talk about it. Poetry was embodied in the act of
seeing and singing, and all the rest was literature. To a request
for a definition of poetry, Lorca replied, "I have fire in my
hands. I understand it and I work with it, but I cannot talk
about it without literature" (p. 95). One recalls Dylan Thomas'
trenchant preface to his collected poems: "These poems . . . are
written for the love of Man and in praise of God, and I'd be a
damn' fool if they weren't." Both statements reveal a distrust
for theorizing about art and a refreshing desire that poems
should be read and enjoyed for their own sake.

From these childhood days, Lorca derived a sense of affinity
with nature that was to bloom into a kind of mythology. His
appeal to the oak tree in 1919 prophesies the man-earth kinship that will soon pulsate in his verse:

¡Hunde en mi pecho tus ramajes santos!,
¡oh solitaria encina,
y deja en mi sub-alma
tus secretos y tu pasión tranquila!

(p. 207)

Sink your holy branches into my breast,
O solitary oak,
and place in my inner heart
your secrets and tranquil passion!

Rooted in the soil of Andalusia, Lorca received the secrets of the oak tree, and they revealed to him in the mysterious phrases of an Iberian sibyl the ancient misery and grief of mankind.

# The Deep Song

"It comes from the first wail
and the first kiss." (p. 1519)

Scattered throughout the record stores of America and Europe are flamenco albums, portraying on their covers a mass of tumbling dark hair, an exultant body, or a trim black silhouette in a Cordobés suit. The original *cante jondo* (or deep song) is not so slick. Its elemental roots, which have been more and more dressed to tourist taste, must be sought off the beaten path in unfrequented Andalusian villages, dark caves sweaty with wine, or, in Lorca's delightful phrase, in the "play of moon and sand" (p. 385).

The composer Manuel de Falla has isolated the sources that, working together, produced this pathetic, monotonous, but heady chant. Byzantine liturgical music contributed markedly through the use of enharmonism, or tones nearly identical in pitch. The repeated insistence on the same note, interspersed with appoggiatura, derives from a Moorish manner of expression. Jewish synagogue chants possess remarkable similarities and probably exercised their share of influence, given the mixed ethnic background of Spain.[9]

9. Manuel de Falla, *Escritos sobre música y músicos* (Madrid: Espasa-Calpe,

Although the *cante jondo* has many variations that seem slight to the uneducated ear, most critics would agree that there are only two basic forms, the *seguiriya* and the *soleá*. The *seguiriya* is generally accepted as the prototype, its four lines clothing great anguish in simple phrases:

> Ar campito solo
> me voy a yorá;
> como tengo yena e pena el arma
> busco soleá.

> To the field alone
> I go to cry;
> since my heart is full of pain
> I hunt for solitude.

The *soleá,* consisting of three lines, delivers a candid epigram, drawn from the ironic and satirical wisdom of the people:

> Anda y con las feas bete,
> que donde está muyo obscuro
> es sol un candil de aceite.[10]

> Go, run with the ugly girls,
> for where it's very dark,
> an oil wick shines like the sun.

Surrounded by a group of gypsies who shout encouragement with resonant *olés* and clap at appropriate times, the singer lets himself go in a frenzy of lament. The unpretentious words are mere foils for the total impact of body and voice. The primitive *cante jondo* often had no guitar to back it up; it was pure vocal emotion. We have Lorca's word that before its emasculation:

---

1950), p. 124. For Jewish roots, see Guillermo Díaz-Plaja, *Federico García Lorca* (Buenos Aires: Espasa-Calpe, 1954), pp. 101–2. In 1922 Falla and Lorca organized a festival of the "deep song" in Granada in order to rescue it from "brothels and evil taverns" (p. 1516). The *cante jondo* existed in Andalusia before the gypsies came in 1452 to add their touches. Today it is these so-called sons of Pharaoh who are its best interpreters.

10. Both examples are from *El cante jondo,* ed. Gabriel María Vergara (Madrid: Hernando, 1922), pp. 13, 52. I have made no attempt to reproduce the gypsy flavor of the language in my translation.

Los viejos
dicen que se erizaban
los cabellos,
y se abría el azogue
de los espejos.
(p. 247)

The old people
say that their hair
stood on end,
the quicksilver split
in the mirrors.

Thus the background of *Poem of the Deep Song (Poema del cante jondo)*, written from 1921 to 1922 but not published until nearly ten years later. A wail (*grito*) like a sheet of sound envelops the book. It begins in the huts or olive groves, spreads to the valleys and plains, enfolds the mountains, becomes identified with the horizon: the *grito* is the poem.

¡Ay!
El grito deja en el viento
una sombra de ciprés.

(Dejadme en este campo
llorando.)

Todo se ha roto en el mundo.
No queda más que el silencio.

(Dejadme en este campo
llorando.)

El horizonte sin luz
está mordido de hogueras.

(Ya os he dicho que me dejéis
en este campo
llorando.)
(pp. 231-32)

*¡Ay!*
The shout leaves in the wind
a shadow of cypress.

(Leave me in this field
to weep.)

Everything in the world is broken.
Only silence is left.

(Leave me in this field
to weep.)

The black horizon
is bitten by bonfires.

(I have begged you to leave me
in this field
to weep.)

The monotonous refrain preserves the touch of the pristine *cante jondo;* the rest is pure Lorca. And it is a battle against silence. The black horizon of grief is "bitten" by shouts arising on all sides. In another poem, the *grito* becomes a "dark rainbow" stretching over the olive fields, the bow of a viola playing the "long strings of the wind." In the end even silence is made resonant:

El silencio

Oye, hijo mío, el silencio.
Es un silencio ondulado,
un silencio,
donde resbalan valles y ecos
y que inclina las frentes
hacia el suelo.

(p. 227)

The Silence

Listen, child: the silence.
It is a wavering silence,
a silence
where valleys and echoes glide,
and foreheads bow
to the ground.

Lorca skillfully adds details of the Andalusian landscape, and fills out the nameless grief its inhabitants have felt for centuries:

Poema de la soleá

Tierra seca,
tierra quieta

de noches
inmensas.

(Viento en el olivar,
viento en la sierra.)

Tierra
vieja
del candil
y la pena.
Tierra
de las hondas cisternas.
Tierra
de la muerte sin ojos
y las flechas.

(Viento por los caminos.
Brisa en las alamedas.)
(p. 229)

Poem of the *Soleá*

Dry earth,
quiet earth
of immense
nights.

(Wind in the olive grove,
wind in the sierra.)

Old
land
of lamp
and grief.
Land
of deep cisterns.
Land
of eyeless death
and arrows.

(Wind on the roads.
A breeze in the poplar groves.)

Death, lurking at the crossroads, suddenly appears, for the
gypsy existence is full of quick violence:

### Sorpresa

Muerto se quedó en la calle
con un puñal en el pecho.
No lo conocía nadie.
¡Cómo temblaba el farol!
Madre.
¡Cómo temblaba el farolito
de la calle!
Era madrugada. Nadie
pudo asomarse a sus ojos
abiertos al duro aire.
Que muerto se quedó en la calle
que con un puñal en el pecho
y que no lo conocía nadie.

(p. 232)

### Surprise

Dead he was left in the street
with a dagger in his chest.
Nobody knew him.
How the lanterns trembled!
Mother of God.
How the little streetlight
trembled!
It was dawn. No one
could peer into his eyes
opened on the harsh air.
Dead he was left in the street
with a dagger in his chest,
and no one knew him.

Only the streetlight reacts to the tragedy—all the rest is the indifference and hardness of death, turning to stone the once vivid, seeing eyes.

The presence of violence creates, in Gustavo Correa's terms, a tremendous tension that is released by the cry, linguistically taking the form of a metaphor. The entire book embodies a desperate urge to communicate and thus to ward off silence. It is a syndrome of communication symbols, including road, cross-roads (cross), arrows, bows, archers, weather vanes, wind, and river. Within this set of symbols, the idea of arrival is equated with communication, and the concept of not arriving (*no llegar*) stands for death. Lorca's poems are populated by horsemen who never reach the end of their journey. Among other death symbols are the stillness of the air, the dryness of the land, the cisterns, the candle and lanterns (always present at a wake), and the ubiquitous knife.[11]

These symbols hover over the crossroads and threaten with extinction the various possibilities of communication implied in the coming together of roads:

Encrucijada

Viento del este:
un farol
y el puñal
en el corazón.
La calle
tiene un temblor
de cuerda
en tensión,
un temblor
de enorme moscardón.
Por todas partes
yo
veo el puñal
en el corazón.

(p. 231)

Crossroads

Wind from the east:
a lantern
and a knife
in the heart.
The street
trembles
like a tense
cord,
buzzes

---

11. *La poesía mítica de Federico García Lorca* (Eugene: University of Oregon Press, 1957), pp. 6, 9–12, 14, 17, 20.

like an enormous fly.
Everywhere
I
see the dagger
in the heart.

A symbol for the singer (*cantaor*) of the deep song is the archer, whose quiver is never empty. Wearing a wide grey hat and trailing a long, slow cape, he comes from the remote land of grief and heads for "the labyrinth of love, crystal, and stone" (p. 235) at the heart of the *cante jondo.*

The real *cante jondo,* said Lorca, belongs to nobody; it floats like thistledown in the winds of time, beyond the reach of literature. Despite this assertion, the *cante jondo* became very much Lorca's property in the twentieth century. Not only did it supply him with the inspiration lacking in his first book, it also responded to his masterful touch, and he was able to turn it into literature without in any way altering its basic feeling. In his lecture in 1922 on the *cante jondo,* he noted the following example of popular grief:

> Yo doy suspiros al aire,
> ¡ay pobrecito de mí!,
> y no los recoge nadie.
>            (p. 1528)

> I scatter sighs in the air,
> oh, wretched me!
> and no one gathers them.

Compare this *soleá* with the first stanza of Lorca's poem "¡Ay!" quoted above:

> El grito deja en el viento
> una sombra de ciprés.

> The shout leaves in the wind
> a shadow of cypress.

Lorca has taken the metaphor of spreading grief in the wind and added to it a dimension of mystery—the shadow of cypress

—which intensifies the sentiment. It is a sophisticated touch, but it does not disturb the original honest simplicity. Furthermore, in the popular songs of Andalusia, Lorca found confirmation of one of his most celebrated techniques, that of giving concrete form to feelings. He noted in his lecture, "It is admirable how in these lyrics a feeling gradually assumes concrete shape. Such is the case with grief (*la pena*). It becomes . . . a dark-haired woman trying to catch birds with the nets of the wind" (pp. 1523–24).

Faced with the elemental brutality of life, the human being raises a cry to the four corners of the earth. This is the nature of the "deep song," an exercise in communication considerably older than European poetry. From this primitive base Lorca developed a modern-day gypsy mythology. But first he had some softer music to play.

# Songs

"The song wishes to be light." (p. 289)

The songs (*Canciones*), written simultaneously with the poems of the *cante jondo,* represent a playful and airy interlude in Lorca's career. The reader is very much reminded of the early poems composed at Granada, except that in the present case impish sensibility expresses itself with more subtlety and sophistication. Snatches from folk lyrics, useless songs for children (the adjective is Lorca's), an occasional tone poem in the provocative *cante jondo* manner, lullabies—these various ingredients are handled with a pristine touch that never appears again in Lorca's work. The poet is taking one last romp in that mountain meadow of his boyhood before violence, tension, and frustration—the chief marks of his adult writing—place their seal on his art forever.

The influence of Juan Ramón Jiménez has been remarked, and the musical, delicate impressionism allows this comparison. But Lorca's eye was more inventive; he gave unique arrangements to surfaces and shapes, light and darkness: in a word, he dared more. Although he has brush strokes that can be as diaphanous as any from the pen of Juan Ramón, their effect is essentially playful:

Paisaje

La tarde equivocada
se vistió de frío.

Detrás de los cristales,
turbios, todos los niños
ven convertirse en pájaros
un árbol amarillo.

La tarde está tendida
a lo largo del río.
Y un rubor de manzana
tiembla en los tejadillos.

(p. 302)

Landscape

The ambiguous afternoon
dressed up in coldness.

Behind the cloudy
windows every child
watched the yellow tree
change into birds.

The afternoon stretched
along the river.
The blush of an apple
trembles on tiny roofs.

Brevity and pithiness characterize much of Spanish literature. The *romance* tradition constantly offers Spanish poets an example of simple, direct expression. To this influence must be added that of the *coplas.* These brief poems of folk origin, usually not more than three or four lines in length, center around the work and play of the people, and are more thoroughly popular than the *romances,* which developed from epic poetry. Unlike the *cante jondo,* which otherwise is quite similar, the *coplas* display less grief, and were sometimes designed for dancing. Ever since they were collected in 1859 by the novelist

Fernán Caballero, they have been the subject of much study in Spain. Lorca, whose art is rooted in popular traditions, could scarcely fail to succumb to their charms.

Many of his *canciones* obviously depart from the example of the *coplas,* but as usual his deft imagination imparts a subtle suggestiveness that is the mark of sophisticated art. Sometimes the suggestion is prompted by the title; on other occasions, there will be a single phrase charged with overtones that greatly increase the connotations of the entire poem. In the following example, Lorca probably intended the title symbolically as well as literally. If we consider the title in connection with the phrase "wounded shadows," we are left with the idea, for which we must supply the details, of something beautiful having been destroyed:

### Cazador

¡Alto pinar!
Cuatro palomas por el aire van.

Cuatro palomas
vuelan y tornan.
Llevan heridas
sus cuatro sombras.

¡Bajo pinar!
Cuatro palomas en la tierra están.

(p. 293)

### Hunter

Lofty pine grove!
Four doves fly by.

Four doves
fly and dive.
They carry four
wounded shadows.

Low pine grove!
Four doves are found on the ground.

Self-evident symbols may be delicately handled with poignant effect. In the following poem, pomegranate trees represent life and cypresses death, as do the sun and moon, respectively. Rarely has the relentless movement of time been shown so daintily and yet so sharply:

Madrigalillo

Cuatro granados
tiene tu huerto.

(Toma mi corazón
nuevo.)

Cuatro cipreses
tendrá tu huerto.

(Toma mi corazón
viejo.)

Sol y luna.
Luego...
¡ni corazón
ni huerto!

(p. 337)

Little Madrigal

Four pomegranate trees
your garden has.

(Take my new
heart.)

Four cypresses
your garden will have.

(Take my old
heart.)

Sun and moon.
And then...
no heart,
no garden!

More than anything, the songs in this book preserve the wonder of being alive, the surprise necessary to poetry. Reading them, one recaptures the pure mystery of objects, the sense of delight that made one shiver as a child and welcome with warm arms life's flow and variety:

De otro modo

La hoguera pone al campo de la tarde
unas astas de ciervo enfurecido.
Todo el valle se tiende. Por sus lomos,
caracolea el vientecillo.

El aire cristaliza bajo el humo.
—Ojo de gato triste y amarillo—.
Yo, en mis ojos, paseo por las ramas.
Las ramas se pasean por el río.

Llegan mis cosas esenciales.
Son estribillos de estribillos.
Entre los juncos y la baja tarde,
¡qué raro que me llame Federico!

(p. 342)

Some Other Way

The bonfire sets in the twilight field
the horns of a furious stag.
All the valley inclines. On its hills,
a gusty wind wheels and prances.

Air crystallizes underneath the smoke.
—Sad and yellow cat's eye—.
I, in my eyes, stroll through the branches.
The branches stroll along the river.

My essential things arrive.
They are refrains of refrains.
Among the reeds and falling afternoon
how strange to be called Federico!

# Gypsy Moon

Lorca spent three years writing and polishing the *Gypsy Bal-lad-Book (Romancero gitano)*, published in 1928. It is one of his few books that appeared in print shortly after its date of composition. To Guillén, he made perfectly clear what he had in mind:

> I am working very hard now. Finishing the "Gypsy Ballads."
> New themes and old suggestions. The Civil Guard comes

and goes through all of Andalusia. . . . "Preciosa y el aire"
is a gypsy ballad, but also a *myth* invented by me. In this
part, I try to harmonize *gypsy mythology* with everyday reality, and the result is strange but I think of new beauty.
I hope to make the images of these people understood by
themselves, visions of the world in which they live. . . .

(p. 1563–64)

Just how much the gypsies understood of Lorca's rare and pungent imagery is hard to say. Nevertheless, the ballads achieved
a tremendous popularity, touching some chord basic to the culture of the Iberian peoples.

The book's inspiration derives in part from Lorca's lively
compassion for the gypsies, who in his time were much tormented by the Civil Guard, a green-uniformed police with pat-
ent leather tri-cornered hats. In the celebrated "Ballad of the
Civil Guard," these implacable guardians of law and order,
their souls as black as their hats and their heads full of a vague
"pistol astronomy," wreak brutal havoc upon a gypsy fiesta (pp.
381–85). To the bourgeoisie of Lorca's time, as now, the gypsies seemed a useless, inferior, good-for-nothing lot. But Lorca
saw in them the elements of poetry and recognized in their di-
sheveled, passionate state a childlike quality. His insight is vin-
dicated by the emotional response we still make to his gypsies,
elevated from rags and misery to "bronze and dreams."

Lorca was able to raise the gypsies to the level of poetry by,
as he put it, inventing a mythology for them. Unlike the sophisticated Greek and Roman myths, the tradition spun by
Lorca's fancy remained close to primitive roots. Reading him
now, we can see that he intuitively evoked in his poetry a primitive ambient that has been explained in formal terms by modern
investigators. Cassirer, basing himself on Frazer, Malinowski,
and Lévy-Bruhl, remarked the close relationship between human reality and cosmic reality in primitive people. It is taken
for granted that the moon, sun, and stars preside over man's
destiny and participate in it. Lorca's great accomplishment in
his gypsy ballads was to revive this magical relationship be-

tween man and the universe, and celebrate what Cassirer called "the consanguinity of all forms of life."[12] In anthropomorphic shapes, the wind, moon, and stars descend to help or hinder man, nature creates a commotion surrounding his acts, and no human being is quite alone in the world.

This closely knit community is ruled over by the moon, baleful queen of lust and death. Robert Graves recently proclaimed her importance for poetry. "Poetry," he said, "began in the matriarchal age, and derives its magic from the moon."[13] No one knew this better than Lorca. The poet Aleixandre paints a revealing picture: "I have seen him late at night, out on some mysterious balcony, as the moon regarded him, silvering his face; and I have felt that his arms were resting on air but that his feet were sunk into time, centuries, the deepest roots of Hispanic earth . . ." (p. 1787). The moon opens the *Gypsy Ballad-Book* by stealing a small boy and closes the book by directing the incestuous love affair between Tamar and Amnon. Her presence continually sends a chill up and down the spine; in Lorca's mythology, she is generally an augur of doom. Later she is explicitly identified with the bull, and thus assumes her complete mythical proportions.[14]

Skillfully mingling music and magic, the famous "Ballad of the Moon" heads the list of songs. Lorca surrounds the death of the gypsy boy with a special atmosphere provided by the

12. *An Essay on Man* (New York: Anchor, 1953), p. 109. See Correa, *La poesía mítica, passim*, for a full and fascinating account of Lorca's mythology. A valuable early effort is by Juan López-Morillas, "García Lorca y el primitivismo lírico: Reflexiones sobre el *Romancero gitano*," *Cuadernos Americanos*, LIII (Sept.–Oct. 1950), 238–50, translated into English in Durán, *Critical Essays*, pp. 130–39.

13. Quoted in J. M. Cohen, *Robert Graves* (London: Oliver and Boyd, Ltd., 1960), pp. 96–97.

14. The influence of the moon on mythology is, of course, incalculable: birth, love, death, and divination come under her spell. In Stone Age culture, she was identified with the bull, an association which stresses, as did Lorca constantly, the similarity between the shape of the crescent moon and the bull's horns. Later, in Egypt, the bull becomes a cow, and is eventually called the Horned Wanderer. See Correa, *La poesía mítica*, p. 164, and also by the same author, "El simbolismo de la luna en la poesía de Federico García Lorca," *PMLA*, LXXII (1957), 1060–84.

moon, who comes down to earth and, supported by the poem's reiterative beat, slowly bewitches the boy with her dancing, and then leads him by the hand into the sky. The images, as always in Lorca, are developed logically, this time from the hard white appearance of the moon. As in the other ballads, the usual translation difficulties are magnified by the repetition of words to form an incantation:

### Romance de la luna, luna

La luna vino a la fragua
con su polisón de nardos.
El niño la mira mira.
El niño la está mirando.
En el aire conmovido
mueve la luna sus brazos
y enseña, lúbrica y pura,
sus senos de duro estaño.

### Ballad of the Moon

The moon came down to the smithy
in her creamy white bustle.
The small boy looks and looks,
and looking watches her still.
In the agitated air
the moon waves her arms,
showing slippery and clear,
her breasts of hard white tin.

Thoroughly captivated, the child warns the moon that the gypsies are about to return and that her whiteness will be made into beads by them:

Huye luna, luna, luna.
Si vinieran los gitanos,
harían con tu corazón
collares y anillos blancos.

Run away, moon, moon, moon.
If the gypsies come,
they'll make from your heart
necklaces and small white rings.

The moon insists on continuing her dance and tells the child
he will soon be sightless. The child repeats his plea for the moon
to flee, and rushes to join her. The moon reprimands him for
treading on her starched bustle:

> Niño, déjame que baile.
> Cuando vengan los gitanos,
> te encontrarán sobre el yunque
> con los ojillos cerrados.
> Huye luna, luna, luna,
> que ya siento sus caballos.
> Niño, déjame, no pises
> mi blancor almidonado.

> Child, let me dance.
> When the gypsies come,
> they'll find you on the anvil
> with your little eyes shut.
> Run away, moon, moon, moon,
> I hear their horses now.
> Child, keep still, don't step on
> my starched whiteness.

Death arrives at the Smithy:

> El jinete se acercaba
> tocando el tambor del llano.
> Dentro de la fragua el niño
> tiene los ojos cerrados.

> The horseman drew near,
> beating the drum of the plain.
> The child inside the forge
> has closed his eyes.

Bathed in an air of myth and moonlight, the gypsies return.
The barn owl (a moon symbol) hoots a sad warning as the
moon and boy trail off through the sky. In a cosmic gesture,
the air joins the gypsy wake:

> Por el olivar venían,
> bronce y sueño, los gitanos.
> Las cabezas levantadas
> y los ojos entornados.

# The Magic of Reality 169

¡Cómo canta la zumaya,
ay cómo canta en el árbol!
Por el cielo va la luna
con un niño de la mano.

Dentro de la fragua lloran,
dando gritos, los gitanos.
El aire la vela, vela,
el aire la está velando.

(pp. 353–54)

Through the olive grove came,
bronzed in dreams, the gypsies.
Their heads uplifted,
their eyes half-closed.

Oh, how the barn owl
whistles in the tree!
Through the sky walks the moon
with a child by the hand.

The gypsies wail and shout
inside the forge.
The air keeps watch,
a careful, careful watch.[15]

Lorca's next creation in his myth-making project was a sylvan encounter between satyr and nymph. The latter is a gypsy girl, and the satyr becomes the anthropomorphized wind and is dubbed "big Saint Christopher." In paintings of the Castilian primitive school, St. Christopher is often pictured as a huge, nearly naked man, towering over rivers and hills, with a small Christ child perched on his shoulder. Something of this image was back of Lorca's name for the lustful pagan "man-wind."

15. The moon has, of course, descended numerous times to the earth in mythology, including the celebrated case of Endymion. In the *Golden Ass* of Apuleius, she appeared carrying an ancient kind of tambourine that made shrill music every time she moved her arms: ". . . in her right hand she had a timbrel of brass, a flat piece of metal carried in the manner of a girdle, wherein passed not many rods through the periphery of it; and when with her arm she moved these triple chords, they gave forth a shrill and clear sound."—Quoted in Robert Graves, *The White Goddess* (New York: Vintage Books, 1958), p. 63. The image is quite close to that of Lorca's moon dancing and waving her arms before the gypsy boy.

As the poem begins, Preciosa, the gypsy nymph, approaches under the fateful sign of the moon (her tambourine). The background of pines and sea responds to her music. Somewhere in the sierras, strange and authoritative, is the house of the English consul, guarded by dozing policemen. As all the world sleeps, Preciosa dances with nature:

### Preciosa y el aire

Su luna de pergamino
Preciosa tocando viene
por un anfibio sendero
de cristales y laureles.
El silencio sin estrellas,
huyendo del sonsonete,
cae donde el mar bate y canta
su noche llena de peces.
En los picos de la sierra
los carabineros duermen
guardando las blancas torres
donde viven los ingleses.
Y los gitanos del agua
levantan por distraerse,
glorietas de caracolas
y ramas de pino verde.

### Preciosa and the Wind

Playing her parchment moon,
Preciosa draws near
along an amphibious path
of crystal and laurel trees.
The starless silence,
fleeing the singsong,
falls where the sea writhes singing
of darkness full of fish.
In the peaks of the sierra
the riflemen doze,
guarding the white towers
where the Englishmen live.
The gypsies of the water
raise for their amusement
bowers of snail shells
and branches of green pine.

Aroused by such sweet music, the lascivious wind, flashing
Freudian tongues of lightning, catches sight of the gypsy girl:

> Su luna de pergamino
> Preciosa tocando viene.
> Al verla se ha levantado
> el viento que nunca duerme.
> San Cristobalón desnudo,
> lleno de lenguas celestes,
> mira a la niña tocando
> una dulce gaita ausente.

> Playing her parchment moon,
> Preciosa draws near.
> The ever-sleepless wind
> on seeing her is stirred.
> Naked big Saint Christopher,
> full of celestial tongues,
> watches the girl playing
> a sweet and absent piper's tune.

The wind brazenly speaks to her:

> Niña, deja que levante
> tu vestido para verte.
> Abre en mis dedos antiguos
> la rosa azul de tu vientre.

> Child, let me lift
> your skirt and look.
> Open in my ancient fingers
> the blue rose of your belly.

All the primitive feeling of sex is embodied in the striking
metaphor of the blue rose and ancient fingers—lust and the
flower to be violated. Preciosa flees in fear, the wind in hot
pursuit. Other elements of nature react to her difficulties, pre-
serving the solidarity of the primitive universe:

> Preciosa tira el pandero
> y corre sin detenerse.
> El viento-hombrón la persigue
> con una espada caliente.

Frunce su rumor el mar.
Los olivos palidecen.
Cantan las flautas de umbría
y el liso gong de la nieve.

.    .    .    .    .    .

Preciosa flings the tambourine
and runs without stopping.
The man-wind pursues her
with his fiery sword.

The sea wrinkles its murmur.
The olive trees grow pale.
The shady flutes are singing,
and the smooth gong of the snow.

.    .    .    .    .    .

Preciosa takes refuge in that tower of civilization and morality,
the home of the English consul, where warm milk and gin offer
little comfort as she babbles her story. Outside, the frustrated
wind howls at the roof:

Preciosa, llena de miedo,
entra en la casa que tiene,
más arriba de los pinos,
el cónsul de los ingleses.

.    .    .    .    .    .

El inglés da a la gitana
un vaso de tibia leche,
y una copa de ginebra
que Preciosa no se bebe.

Y mientras cuenta, llorando,
su aventura a aquella gente,
en las tejas de pizarra
el viento, furioso, muerde.

(PP. 354–56)

Preciosa, filled with dread,
goes into the house that belongs,
high above the pines,
to the consul of the English.

.    .    .    .    .    .

The Englishman offers her
a glass of warm milk,
and a tot of gin
that Preciosa does not touch.

And while she tells, with sobs,
her adventure to all those people,
at the roof of slate
the wind is gnawing in fury.

After the mythical adventure, the commonplace elements in these stanzas provide a flat contrast that Lorca quickly eliminates with his final image of the wind.

Once again Lorca has drawn, consciously or unconsciously, from the well of folklore. The wind as a violator of women is a part of folk legend in Australia and among the North American Indians. We need only recall that Hiawatha's father was the West Wind. In the Spanish province of Asturias, unmarried girls still avoid a brisk breeze.[16] Whether or not Lorca knew this superstition, there are frequent echoes of it in his poetry. A lovely girl, picking olives in Andalusia, refuses the offers of all passing men. She prefers the long, grey arm of the wind wrapped around her waist (p. 310).

Lunar influence looms large again in Lorca's most widely discussed poem, the "Sleep-Walking Ballad" ("Romance sonámbulo"). Story, myth, and dream weave a magical pattern in this tale of a wounded smuggler's search for his sweetheart, a gypsy girl lost in the arms of the moon as she stands trancelike upon her balcony. The duality of dream and reality is adroitly balanced throughout.

The famous opening lines are an incantation to suggest the

16. See Stith Thompson, *The Folktale* (New York: Dryden, 1946), p. 307, and Enrique Casas Gaspar, *Costumbres españolas de nacimiento, noviazgo, casamiento y muerte* (Madrid: Escelicer, 1947), p. 20. German legend recognizes the wind as the wild huntsman in pursuit of the maiden (Jung, *The Psychology of the Unconscious* [New York: Moffart, Yard & Co., 1916], p. 312). Lorca insisted that Preciosa was his own myth, despite the obvious parallel to Boreas and Orithyia (see Ovid's *Metamorphoses*, vi, 682 ff). Amado Alonso believed that Lorca did have Ovid in mind. See Charles H. Leighton, "The Treatment of Time and Space in the *Romancero gitano*," *Hispania*, XLIII (1960), 378–83.

spell of the moon as it bathes everything in a green and silver
glow. The ship and horse are implements of the smuggler's
trade. They are also anchor symbols for reality. They end the
poem, and apparently escape the moon's green spell. Underneath the gypsy moon, objects gaze at the girl, but she cannot
gaze back, suggesting the temporary suspension or confusion of
the vital sense of sight, as one would expect in a somnabulant
state.

### Romance sonámbulo

Verde que te quiero verde.
Verde viento. Verdes ramas.
El barco sobre la mar
y el caballo en la montaña.
Con la sombra en la cintura
ella sueña en su baranda,
verde carne, pelo verde,
con ojos de fría plata.
Verde que te quiero verde.
Bajo la luna gitana,
las cosas la están mirando
y ella no puede mirarlas.

### Sleep-Walking Ballad

Green I love you green.
Green wind. Green branches.
The ship upon the ocean
and the horse upon the mountain.
With shadow around her waist
she dreams upon her balcony,
green flesh, green hair,
with eyes of chill silver.
Green I love you green.
Underneath the gypsy moon
all things look upon her
but she cannot look back.

Once again nature stirs portentously, a fig tree moves harshly
against the wind. Someone is coming, but the girl in her moon
spell is oblivious:

Verde que te quiero verde.
Grandes estrellas de escarcha,
vienen con el pez de sombra
que abre el camino del alba.
La higuera frota su viento
con la lija de sus ramas,
y el monte, gato garduño,
eriza sus pitas agrias.
¿Pero quién vendrá? ¿Y por dónde...?
Ella sigue en su baranda,
verde carne, pelo verde,
soñando en la mar amarga.

Green I love you green.
Great frosty stars
arrive with the shadowy fish
that opens the road of dawn.
The fig tree rubs the wind
with the sandpaper of its branches,
and the mountain, a furtive cat,
bristles its sour cactus.
But who is coming? And from where...?
She lingers upon her balcony,
green flesh, green hair,
dreaming of the bitter sea.

The bleeding smuggler arrives and asks the girl's father for rest and shelter. The latter would comply but, as in a dream, he is no longer master of himself (or, in terms of reality, he is afraid to protect a hunted man). Three hundred brown roses stand for the dried blood on the fleeing man's shirt. He begs at least to climb the balcony to the moon and girl:

Compadre, quiero cambiar
mi caballo por su casa,
mi montura por su espejo,
mi cuchillo por su manta.
Compadre, vengo sangrando,
desde los puertos de Cabra.
Si yo pudiera, mocito,
ese trato se cerraba.
Pero yo ya no soy yo,

ni mi casa es ya mi casa.
　Compadre, quiero morir
decentemente en mi cama.
De acero, si puede ser,
con las sábanas de holanda.
¿No ves la herida que tengo
desde el pecho a la garganta?
　Trescientas rosas morenas
lleva tu pechera blanca.
Tu sangre rezuma y huele
alrededor de tu faja.
Pero yo ya no soy yo,
ni mi casa es ya mi casa.
　Dejadme subir al menos
hasta las altas barandas,
¡dejadme subir!, dejadme
hasta las verdes barandas.
Barandales de la luna
por donde retumba el agua.


　"Friend, I want to change
my horse for your house,
my mount for your mirror,
my knife for your blanket.
Friend, I have come bleeding
from the pass of Cabra."
　"If I could, my lad,
I would make that trade.
But I am no longer I,
nor is my house now my house."
　"Friend, I want to die
decently in my bed.
Of steel, if it can possibly be,
with sheets of finespun linen.
Don't you see the wound I carry
from my breast to my throat?"
　"Three hundred dark roses
Your white shirt bears.
Your blood oozes pungently
around your sash.
But I am no longer I,
nor is my house now my house."
　"Let me climb, at least,

up to the high balcony,
let me go up! let me
up to the green balcony.
The balcony of the moon
where the water pounds."

The two climb together, leaving a trail of blood and tears. The
roofs tremble, and a thousand tambourines rattle with the arrival of dawn:

> Ya suben los dos compadres
> hacia las altas barandas.
> Dejando un rastro de sangre.
> Dejando un rastro de lágrimas.
> Temblaban en los tejados
> farolillos de hojalata.
> Mil panderos de cristal
> herían la madrugada.

> Now the two friends climb
> up to the high balcony.
> Leaving a trail of blood.
> Leaving a trail of tears.
> Trembling over the roofs
> were little lanterns of tin.
> A thousand tambourines of glass
> pierced the dawn.

The search for the girl continues on the high balcony of the
moon. Before she fell under the lunar spell, her face was fresh
and her hair black:

> Verde que te quiero verde,
> verde viento, verdes ramas.
> Los dos compadres subieron.
> El largo viento dejaba
> en la boca un raro gusto
> de hiel, de menta y de albahaca.
> ¡Compadre! ¿Dónde está, dime?
> ¿Dónde está tu niña amarga?
> ¡Cuántas veces te esperó!
> ¡Cuántas veces te esperara,
> cara fresca, negro pelo,
> en esta verde baranda!

Green I love you green,
green wind, green branches.
The two friends have ascended.
The long wind left
in their mouths a strange taste
of gall, mint, and sweet basil.
    "Friend! Tell me, where is she?
Where is your bitter daughter?"
    "How often she waited for you!
How often she would wait for you,
face fresh, hair black,
upon this green balcony!"

Now the previous elements of the poem come together. The
gypsy girl is completely identified with the moonlight. As when
one awakens from sleep, the night becomes intimate. The Civil
Guard hammers at the door, and the poem closes with its opening refrain, a mixture of dream and reality:

Sobre el rostro del aljibe
se mecía la gitana.
Verde carne, pelo verde,
con ojos de fría plata.
Un carámbano de luna
la sostiene sobre el agua.
La noche se puso íntima
como una pequeña plaza.
Guardias civiles borrachos
en la puerta golpeaban.
Verde que te quiero verde.
Verde viento. Verdes ramas.
El barco sobre la mar.
Y el caballo en la montaña.
                    (pp. 358–60)

Above the cistern face
swayed the gypsy girl.
Green flesh, green hair,
with eyes of chill silver.
An icicle of moon
holds her over the water.
The night has become intimate
like a little plaza.

> Drunken civil guards
> were beating at the door.
> Green I love you green.
> Green wind. Green branches.
> The ship upon the ocean.
> And the horse upon the mountain.

Freudian analysis could be applied to this ballad, with its balconies and staircases, its icicle and cistern, and efforts to ascend. The now-familiar mechanism of dreams—the condensation of meaning and displacement of accent—is clearly apparent in much of Lorca. In this dream ballad, the smuggler wants to trade his horse, saddle, and knife (all masculine symbols of aggressiveness and vitality) for a house, mirror, and blanket (all symbols of femininity, receptiveness, and peace). I leave it to the analysts to draw their own conclusions; however, a great deal of light could be thrown on Lorca by means of such probing.

The brilliant sensual metaphors of the gypsy ballads are justly famous. A poet must be a professor of the five senses, said Lorca, sight first and then touch. In a country where official prudishness is nearly always hypocrisy, Lorca cut through social standards with shocking ease. His work fastens upon the human body, so often absent or sublimated in Spanish poetry, and celebrates the flesh as a source of song.

The well-known and oft-quoted ballad, "The Faithless Wife" ("La casada infiel") describes the sexual act in terms of ancient symbols of flower, fish, and horse:

> Ni nardos ni caracolas
> tienen el cutis tan fino,
> ni los cristales con luna
> relumbran con ese brillo.
> Sus muslos se me escapaban
> como peces sorprendidos,
> la mitad llenos de lumbre,
> la mitad llenos de frío.
> Aquella noche corrí
> el mejor de los caminos,
> montado en potra de nácar
> sin bridas y sin estribos.
>
> (p. 363)

> Neither tuberose nor sea shell
> has such a fine skin,
> nor do mirrors in moonlight
> shine with such a glow.
> Her thighs escaped me
> like startled fish,
> half full of light,
> half full of cold.
> That night I traveled
> the best of roads,
> mounted on a pony of pearl,
> free of bridle or stirrup.

With unerring accuracy Lorca fastened on the fish and shell as sexual symbols. They are, in this respect, as old as mankind.[17] Knives also gleam like fish, and in *Blood Wedding* the condensation is complete when the knife becomes a "fish without scales or river" (p. 1182).

In the incestuous ballad "Tamar and Amnon," a marvelous synthesis of sexual symbols is achieved:

> Thamar, en tus pechos altos
> hay dos peces que me llaman,
> y en las yemas de tus dedos
> rumor de rosa encerrada.
>
> (p. 394)
>
> Tamar, in your high breasts
> are two fishes calling me,
> and in the tips of your fingers
> a murmur of sealed roses.

# The Broken Compass

> "And every island fled away, and
> the mountains were not found."
> Revelation XVI:20

Lorca arrived in New York in the summer of 1929 in search of a complete change. Clamorous success had attended the publication of the *Gypsy Ballad-Book* a year before, and,

17. "Oysters, shells . . . and pearls . . . partake of sexual symbolism . . . , of the sacred powers concentrated in water, moon, and woman . . . , of the

by leaving Spain, he sought to dissociate himself from the implications of its success, fearing he would be permanently labeled as a poet of "barbarous" themes.

The change provided by New York proved to be cataclysmal. No sharper contrast can be imagined than that between rural, agrarian, and tradition-bound Spain and the roaring twenties of New York. Lorca came from the land which had heard Unamuno shout, "Let others invent!" to the country ostensibly in the forefront of the industrial revolution.

More than any other happening in the long evolution of mankind (even more than the development of rationalism), industrial society is responsible for destroying the close, vital relationship between man and the cosmos that Lorca had evoked in his gypsy ballads. The advent of the machine age and the metropolis effectively established the here and now of man, underlining his responsibility and his aloneness. In terms of the magical style of Lorca's poetry, there could be no bond between New York and the cosmos. The moon, wind, sun, and stars would not deign to mingle with the prosaic-minded inhabitants of this immense city which had competently displayed its independence from nature and was attempting to control it. Reversing the rôle of the American innocent abroad in a sophisticated cultured, and cynical Europe, Lorca became the vulnerable European from a "backward" country, peculiarly unprepared by temperament as well as nationality for New York's modernity. The magic, delicate, primitive house of his poetry came tumbling down.

*Poet in New York* is a description of this collapse and of the painful process of picking up the pieces. The personal intervention of natural and mythical elements provided the gypsy with a sense of design and inspired his life with awe. In New York this sense of order crumbles, and chaos prevails. Mythical figures are systematically assassinated by negative symbols. The prevalent concepts are "hollow" (*hueco*) and

---

magic power of the uterus."—Mircea Eliade, *Imágenes y símbolos*, trans. Carmen Castro (Madrid: Taurus, 1955), pp. 137, 140.

"vacuum" (*vacío*). Everywhere the exuberant warmth of the gypsy ballads is replaced by the impersonal coldness of the New York herds; impending catastrophe is suggested by the symbols of shipwreck (*naufragio*), dance of death, and destruction of planets. The sea and snow, pulled out of their natural context, are prime tokens of that fearful silence against which the *cante jondo* had intuitively risen.[18]

Although a baneful influence in the gypsy ballads, the moon, nevertheless, was filled with mythic grandeur. She was still the goddess with whom, according to Pliny, all things wax or wane. In *Poet in New York,* we watch her systematic decline, first into symbols of stagnation and horror—sharp bone splinters, a horse's skull; and finally into the degradation of the fat woman, a pathetic Preciosa passing through a sick multitude. The moon has lost its mythical force:

> La mujer gorda venía delante
> arrancando las raíces y mojando el pergamino de los tambores;
> la mujer gorda
> que vuelve del revés los pulpos agonizantes.
> La mujer gorda, enemiga de la luna,
> corría por las calles y los pisos deshabitados.
>
>                                 (p. 415)

> The fat woman led the way,
> pulling up roots and wetting the drums' parchment;
> the fat woman,
> turning over the flailing octopus.
> The fat woman, enemy of the moon,
> ran through the streets and empty apartments.

Utter rootlessness is a consequence of the breakdown of the mythical structure, forcing a desperate search for identity both personal and formal. Even things themselves are false and without orientation, a terrible calamity for Lorca, since he drew inspiration directly from concrete objects:

> He visto que las cosas
> cuando buscan su curso encuentran su vacío.
>                         (p. 400)

18. Correa, *La poesía mítica,* pp. 115–26, 145–46.

> I have seen that things
> when they seek their course encounter their vacuum.

Facelessness is a prime indication of lack of identity. Also, suits (*trajes*) represent a mask covering spontaneity. The chief nightmare of New York is a "swarm of suits without heads" (p. 410). And the Chinaman who cannot find the nakedness of his wife (p. 413) stands for the impossibility of intimate relationship in urban living. Even the anguish of New York is imperfect (p. 415) because it is not natural.

The first line of the book forces upon us the sense of Lorca's lost direction, his "broken compass":

> Asesinado por el cielo,
> entre las formas que van hacia la sierpe
> y las formas que buscan el cristal,
> dejaré caer mis cabellos.
>
> (p. 399)

> Assassinated by the sky,
> between forms that flow towards the serpent
> and forms that search for glass,
> I shall let fall my hair.

The serpent is the subway, and the glass the office buildings. These were foreign goals to Lorca, but the heart of the matter is that he has been struck down by what should have been a familiar signpost, the sky.

These first poems are concerned with a lyrical crisis. Childhood keeps struggling to return, but everywhere it is drowned by the noisy reality of New York. As a result, it is not until halfway through the book that he gains a firm grasp on his technique and channels the violent flood of surrealistic imagery into a meaningful direction.

Amidst this welter of facelessness and repressed emotions, Lorca's first act was to find a substitute for his gypsies. The Negro, too, was a primitive soul, persecuted by an entire class, and kept from being a child of nature by the artificial canyons towering above him. Lorca responded immediately, but he could not create a Negro myth. It was primitivism outside a

tradition, and this made all the difference. The olive-colored
gypsies belonged in their caves and on the beaches of Andalusia; the black man did not belong in apartments or subways.
The struggle to fuse primitive and mechanical elements left
only a sense of frenzy:

> El ímpetu primitivo baila con el ímpetu mecánico,
> ignorantes en su frenesí de la luz original.

(p. 413)

> The primitive impulse dances with the mechanical impulse,
> both in their frenzy ignorant of original light.

At all events, the Negro became the first sympathetic element in Lorca's New York poetry. Perhaps the doorman at
John Jay Hall, Columbia University, inspired "Ode to the King
of Harlem." In the ludicrous actions of the first stanza, there
is a reflection of the now-debased myth-maker and also of the
ridiculous position of an African native tending doors for New
York students:

> Con una cuchara,
> arrancaba los ojos a los cocodrilos
> y golpeaba el trasero de los monos.

> With a spoon
> he dug out the crocodiles' eyes
> and spanked the monkeys on their behinds.

What follows is a surrealistic treatment of the race question,
a systematic effort to abolish whiteness as symbolized in the
blond brandy-seller, the apple, the color of sand, and the white
beans (*judías*).[19] In opposition are the king and his crocodiles,
and all the implements of servitude in the white man's house:

19. *Judía* translates the various beans belonging to the *phaseolus* family:
kidney, Lima, and string beans. It also means "Jewess," and Ben Belitt has
rendered it this way in his translation of Lorca's *Poet in New York* (New
York: Grove Press, 1955), p. 19. I have preferred the meaning of "white
beans," since it carries through the obvious sense of whiteness begun by the
blond brandy-seller, and since the bubbles (*burbujas*) could also refer to the
shape and color of the beans. Lorca remarked to a friend the Negro's ". . . vain
efforts to bury all traces of his race under a mask of pomade and cosmetics"
(Belitt, *Poet in New York*, p. 183).

Es preciso matar al rubio vendedor de aguardiente,
a todos los amigos de la manzana y de la arena,
y es necesario dar con los puños cerrados
a las pequeñas judías que tiemblan llenas de burbujas,
para que el rey de Harlem cante con su muchedumbre,
para que los cocodrilos duerman en largas filas
bajo el amianto de la luna,
y para que nadie dude de la infinita belleza
de los plumeros, los ralladores, los cobres y las cacerolas de
      las cocinas.

Kill the blond brandy-seller,
and all the friends of apple and sand,
and beat with closed fists
the little white beans that tremble full of bubbles,
so that the king of Harlem may sing with his multitude,
and the crocodiles sleep in long rows
underneath the asbestos moon,
that no one may doubt the infinite beauty
of dusters and graters, of kitchen brass and casseroles.

Then, with a tone reminiscent of the *Gypsy Ballads,* Lorca exalts the suffering of New York's Negroes:

¡Ay Harlem! ¡Ay Harlem! ¡Ay Harlem!
¡No hay angustia comparable a tus ojos oprimidos,
a tu sangre estremecida dentro del eclipse oscuro,
a tu violencia granate sordomuda en la penumbra,
a tu gran rey prisionero con un traje de conserje!

O Harlem, Harlem, Harlem!
There is no anguish like your oppressed eyes,
or your blood shuddering in its dark eclipse,
or your stone-red, deaf-dumb violence in the half-shadow,
or your great king a prisoner in his doorman's uniform!

The symbols of vitality common to Lorca's verse (eyes, blood, song) are abused in Harlem. The Negroes' blood seeks doors, cracks, crannies—outlets of any kind to whiteness and freedom; it tries to burn the chlorophyll of blonde women or hunts for flour-covered death and tuberose ashes (p. 408). Dammed-up blood becomes the symbol of blocked poetry, for Lorca, too, was threatened by facelessness and disguise. Across the amputated symbols of natural life, the warm, vital murmur of the Negroes reached Lorca's heart:

> ¡Ay Harlem disfrazada!
> ¡Ay, Harlem, amenazada por un gentío de trajes sin cabeza!
> Me llega tu rumor,
> me llega tu rumor atravesando troncos y ascensores,
> a través de láminas grises,
> donde flotan tus automóviles cubiertos de dientes,
> a través de los caballos muertos y los crímenes diminutos,
> a través de tu gran rey desesperado,
> cuyas barbas llegan al mar.
>
> (pp. 406–10)

> O disguised Harlem!
> O Harlem, threatened by a swarm of suits without faces!
> Your murmur reaches me,
> your murmur reaches me across tree trunks and elevators,
> over grey slates
> where your teeth-covered automobiles float,
> through dead horses and minute crimes,
> through your great and desperate king,
> whose beard trails to the sea.

But mostly New York was anguish. In the face of it, he could only proclaim the perpetual wakefulness of live flesh, still surrounded by such negative symbols as snow and dead dahlias:

> No duerme nadie por el cielo. Nadie, nadie.
> No duerme nadie.
>
> .    .    .    .    .    .    .
>
> No es sueño la vida. ¡Alerta! ¡Alerta! ¡Alerta!
> Nos caemos por las escaleras para comer la tierra húmeda
> o subimos al filo de la nieve con el coro de las dalias muertas.
> Pero no hay olvido, ni sueño;
> carne viva. Los besos atan las bocas
> en una maraña de venas recientes
> y al que le duele su dolor le dolerá sin descanso
> y al que teme la muerte la llevará sobre sus hombros.
>
> (pp. 420–21)

No one sleeps in the heavens. No one, no one.
No one sleeps.

.    .    .    .    .    .    .    .    .

Life is not a dream. Look out! Watch out!
We fall downstairs to eat the humid earth
or we climb the edge of snow with the choir of dead dahlias.
But there is no oblivion, nor sleep;
live flesh. Kisses tie up mouths
in a tangle of fresh veins,
and he whose pain hurts him, it will hurt forever,
and he who fears death will bear it on his shoulders.

With the arrival of summer, Lorca left the city for the New
England countryside. There the soft and pleasant greenness
released the tension that had been cruelly bending him down.
The "Poems of Lake Eden Mills" (Vermont) reveal a personal, pathetic glimpse such as we have not had since the early
poems of 1918. Nature at once summoned the lyric voice of
his youth, which strives to rise from the ferns lying at his feet
before being devoured by the horse's teeth:

Era mi voz antigua
ignorante de los densos jugos amargos.
La adivino lamiendo mis pies
bajo los frágiles helechos mojados.

¡Ay voz antigua de mi amor,
ay voz de mi verdad,
ay voz de mi abierto costado,
cuando todas las rosas manaban de mi lengua
y el césped no conocía la impasible dentadura del caballo!

.    .    .    .    .    .    .    .    .

¡Oh voz antigua, quema con tu lengua
esta voz de hojalata y de talco!

It was my old voice
ignorant of the thick and bitter juices.
I divine it licking my feet
under the fragile wet ferns.

Old voice of my love,
voice of my truth,

voice of my opened ribs,
when roses flowed from my tongue
and the lawn did not know the impassive horse's teeth!

.    .    .    .    .    .    .    .    .    .    .

Old voice, burn with your tongue
this voice of tinfoil and tinsel!

The overwhelming knowledge that he is forever separated
from his youth makes him want to weep like a neglected child.
Coupled with this is the profound realization that words now
intrude between him and the primitive synthesis he so successfully evoked in the *Gypsy Ballad-Book*. If he wishes to be as
a rose, a child, and a tree, then he must suppress his constant
verbal juggling. Lorca plunged deeply into the entangled relationship between words and emotions, and emerged with a
telling image of the poet as a wounded pulse probing the mystery of life:

> Quiero llorar porque me da la gana
> como lloran los niños del último banco,
> porque yo no soy un hombre, ni un poeta, ni una hoja,
> pero sí un pulso herido que sonda las cosas del otro lado.
>
> Quiero llorar diciendo mi nombre,
> rosa, niño y abeto a la orilla de este lago,
> para decir mi verdad de hombre de sangre
> matando en mí la burla y la sugestión del vocablo.
>
> (pp. 426–27)

> I want to cry because I feel like it,
> the way children in the back row cry,
> because I am not a man, or a poet, or a leaf,
> but instead a wounded pulse probing things from the other
>     side.
>
> I want to cry, saying my name,
> rose, child, spruce tree on the shore of this lake,
> in order to tell my truth as a man of blood,
> suppressing in myself jest and the word's suggestion.

This poem is the turning point of Lorca's New York experience. Having reached the nadir of his emotional crisis,
he began slowly to ascend to the new fame of poet-dramatist

awaiting him. Once back in the city, there is a stronger sense of direction and a more knowing denunciation of metropolitan living, based upon man's inhumanity to man:

Yo denuncio a toda la gente
que ignora la otra mitad,
la mitad irredimible
que levanta sus montes de cemento
donde laten los corazones
de los animalitos que se olvidan
y donde caeremos todos
en la última fiesta de los taladros.

. . . . . .

Hay un mundo de ríos quebrados
y distancias inasibles
en la patita de ese gato
quebrada por el automóvil,
y yo oigo el canto de la lombriz
en el corazón de muchas niñas.

(pp. 444–45)

I denounce all people
who ignore the other half,
the unregenerate half
who raise their cement mountains
where beat the hearts
of small forgotten animals
and where we shall all fall
in the final feast of the drills.

. . . . . .

There is a world of broken rivers
and untouchable distances
in that kitten's paw
crushed by the automobile,
and I hear the song of the earthworm
in the heart of many small girls.

Under the guidance of compassion, the startling images coincide with a tone of moral outrage, and an affirmative symbol appears: the spike of wheat, representing a return to natural life and mythical significance. At the conclusion of the long ode to Walt Whitman, which decries the perversion of natural impulses, Lorca pleads for the coming of a new kingdom, heralded by a Negro child:

> Quiero que el aire fuerte de la noche más honda
> quite flores y letras del arco donde duermes
> y un niño anuncie a los blancos del oro
> la llegada del reino de la espiga.

(p. 454)

> I want the strong air of deepest night
> to lift the flowers and letters from the arch where you sleep
> and a Negro child to announce to white men and their gold
> the coming of the kingdom of the spike of wheat.

Lorca's Manhattan is inhabited by broken objects, hapless creatures, demons, and jungle animals. This bizarre conglomeration has interfered with a true appreciation of the value of *Poet in New York,* a value heightened by the book's inspired compassion and the fact that it contains some of the best surrealistic poetry ever written.

In his relations with surrealism, Lorca preserved his usual autonomy. He may have heard a lecture by Louis Aragon in 1925 at the Residencia in Madrid where he lived. Parts of *Poet in New York* show a familiarity with French surrealism.[20] But Lorca's passionate dismay and aroused tone of indignation is far removed from the intellectual calculation of the surrealist movement, and he avoids the exhibitionistic element so enjoyed by the Parisian poets. Aragon had urged that each image be a re-examination of the world, but Lorca had been doing that ever since the *cante jondo* poems, and with decided control and aesthetic concern. He allowed automatic association, but kept it in logical touch with concrete reality. The serpents and wild beasts roaming through these poems, for example, are the result of frequent visits to the New York zoo, where he was drawn in search of naturalness, only to find it behind bars.

20. Del Río, *Poeta en Nueva York,* p. 38. The author discusses probable literary influences on Lorca in New York. Lorca read Dos Passos, Erich Maria Remarque, and possibly T. S. Eliot, all in Spanish translations. Through León Felipe, translator of Whitman, he became acquainted with the tone of Whitman without necessarily having read him, as was his manner. He was also quite interested in Negro spirituals (*ibid.,* pp. 35–38).

Like all of Lorca, *Poet in New York* is a revision of surrounding reality, with, in this case, the introduction of surrealistic techniques that receded when he returned to Spain.

# The Terrible Mothers

"Now the dove and leopard struggle." (p. 465)

In 1934 Lorca's good friend and fellow poet was fatally gored
in the bull ring. "Lament for Ignacio Sánchez Mejías," written in a spasm of deep grief soon after the savage moment is
generally considered to be the culmination of Lorca's talents,
as well as one of the finest of modern elegies.

The background of an ancient national spectacle provided
Lorca with the opportunity to revive his rôle as myth-maker.
Lecturing on daemonic inspiration in art a few months before
Ignacio's tragic accident, Lorca had shown himself to be keenly
aware of the mythological significance of the bullfight. Those
who dismiss the *corrida de toros* as tasteless butchery, he said,
overlook the fact that the death of the bull is a ritual sacrifice
performed by the bullfighter, who is the modern incarnation of
a primordial priest. In such a context, Lorca placed the death
of his friend. Ignacio fell by the horns of the bull in the final
act of a meaningless ritual that is intimately associated with
the human race's ancient need for sacrifice in order to purify
itself. Ignacio's death is that of the hero's.

No longer maimed and helpless as they were in New York,
the mythological protagonists of Lorca's poetry return to act
as governors of man's destiny. Death rides upon the horns of
the bull, which by their shape suggest the half-moon and her
sinister influence. Ignacio's end is not the pitiless, almost impersonal, exit of a man struck down by an automobile; instead,
it acquires primitive terror and grandeur. By exalting a native
tradition, Lorca purged his emotions and at the same time
reached the hearts of all men.

The elegy is in four parts, each one expressing a different
sentiment. The first part, treating of the goring and death, is
a dirge: the second part, in which the bull is given mythical

status along with the sacrificial blood, approximates the *cante jondo* manner; in Part 3, faced with the supreme fact of Ignacio's body upon a stone slab, the poet reverts to formal alexandrine verse; and in Part 4, the final eulogy of the departed hero, he chooses an eleven-syllable line of Petrarchian origin. In the last two stanzas, the alexandrines reappear, to clothe a simple, haunting tribute. On the basis of structure alone, the "Lament" suggests that Lorca is one of the most formidable poets of his time.

    *Part 1:* "The Goring and Death" ("La cogida y la muerte"). With the dreadful insistence of a funeral bell summoning the populace to mourning, one phrase is repeated in every other line: "At five in the afternoon" ("A las cinco de la tarde"). A small boy symbolically brings the winding sheet, the coffin is ready, and death takes command:

> A las cinco de la tarde.
> Eran las cinco en punto de la tarde.
> Un niño trajo la blanca sábana
> *a las cinco de la tarde.*
> Una espuerta de cal ya prevenida
> *a las cinco de la tarde.*
> Lo demás era muerte y sólo muerte
> *a las cinco de la tarde.*
>
> (p. 465)

> At five in the afternoon.
> It was exactly five in the afternoon.
> A boy brought the white sheet
> *at five in the afternoon.*
> A basket of lime was ready
> *at five in the afternoon.*
> All else was death and only death
> *at five in the afternoon.*

The commotion attending death fills the rest of this part, punctuated in every other line by the mournful refrain. Cotton flies in the wind; a coffin on wheels suggests the emergency operating room, while death lays eggs in the wound, presaging the arrival of gangrene. A combat between the dove and the leop-

ard symbolizes innocence struggling with evil. Ignacio is dead,
and the bell continues to toll with terrible insistence:

> ¡Ay qué terribles cinco de la tarde!
> ¡Eran las cinco en todos los relojes!
> ¡Eran las cinco en sombra de la tarde!
> (p. 466)

> What a terrible five in the afternoon!
> It was five on every clock!
> It was five in the shade of the afternoon!

*Part 2:* "The Spilled Blood" ("La sangre derramada").
After the sacrifice of the bull in ancient times, a fortunate
young man was often permitted to bathe in its blood, emerging
cleansed and renewed.[21] In the present case, the spilled blood,
being that of the bullfighter-priest, is ambivalent. The life
symbol that sought an outlet in *Poet in New York* is here
wasted on the ground. Lorca refuses to look at it, and calls for
the moon, whose presence will supposedly overwhelm the scene.
The bull is presented in such a way as to stir the reader with
primeval associations:

> La vaca del viejo mundo
> pasaba su triste lengua
> sobre un hocico de sangres
> derramadas en la arena,
> y los toros de Guisando,
> casi muerte y casi piedra,
> mugieron como dos siglos
> hartos de pisar la tierra.
> No.
> ¡Que no quiero verla!
> (p. 467–68)

> The cow of the old world
> licked with her sad tongue
> a snoutful of blood
> spilled upon the sand,
> and the bulls of Guisando,
> partly death and partly stone,

21. Sir James Frazer, quoted in Correa, *La poesía mítica*, p. 165, n. 30.

bellowed with the sound of two hundred years,
weary of trampling the earth.
No.
I do not want to see it!

Ignacio climbs the tiers, death weighing on his shoulders as
he seeks the dawn no longer his. Another reference to the bull
evokes a terrible female presence, related to the ancient goddess
of death and lust celebrated by Robert Graves:

> No se cerraron sus ojos
> cuando vio los cuernos cerca,
> pero las madres terribles
> levantaron la cabeza.
>
> (p. 468)

> His eyes did not close
> when he saw the horns near,
> but the terrible mothers
> raised their heads.

No prince of Seville could compare with this *torero,* who carried himself with Roman dignity. But his blood is spattered
upon the sand, and the inconceivability of this fact underlies
the imagery of the closing lines in this section:

> Que no hay cáliz que la contenga,
> que no hay golondrinas que se la beban,
> no hay escarcha de luz que la enfríe,
> no hay canto ni diluvio de azucenas,
> no hay cristal que la cubra de plata.
> No.
> ¡¡Yo no quiero verla!!
>
> (p. 470)

> There is no chalice to contain it,
> there are no swallows to drink it,
> no shining frost to freeze it,
> no song nor shower of lilies,
> no crystal to cover it with silver.
> No.
> I do not want to see it!!

*Part 3:* "In the Presence of the Body" ("El cuerpo presente"). Confronted with the harsh conclusion of Ignacio's life

upon a mortuary slab, the poem reverts to the symbolic struggle between leopard and dove begun in Part 1 and now continued in terms of a contest between water (vitality) and stone
(death). The slab is impassive before all forms of life: dreams
moan without, seeking admittance; the tender arms of grey
rain avoid dashing against its surface:

> La piedra es una frente donde los sueños gimen
> sin tener agua curva ni cipreses helados.
> La piedra es una espalda para llevar al tiempo
> con árboles de lágrimas y cintas y planetas.
>
> Yo he visto lluvias grises correr hacia las olas
> levantando sus tiernos brazos acribillados
> para no ser cazadas por la piedra tendida
> que desata sus miembros sin empapar la sangre.
> (p. 470)

> The stone is a forehead where dreams moan without,
> lacking the curve of water and frozen cypresses.
> The stone is a broad back that carries time
> with trees of tears and ribbons and planets.
>
> I have seen grey rain run towards the waves,
> raising its tender riddled arms
> so as not to be hounded by the outstretched stone
> that undoes limbs without absorbing blood.

Ignacio "the well-born" lies on the flat stone, his head assuming the shape of a minotaur in homage to his slayer. Water
(life) seeks him. It penetrates his mouth but is not tasted.
Decay begins: the nightingales (blood) are replaced by bottomless holes:

> Ya se acabó. La lluvia penetra por su boca.
> El aire como loco deja su pecho hundido,
> y el amor, empapado con lágrimas de nieve,
> se calienta en la cumbre de las ganaderías.
>
> ¿Qué dicen? Un silencio con hedores reposa.
> Estamos con un cuerpo presente que se esfuma,
> con una forma clara que tuvo ruiseñores
> y la vemos llenarse de agujeros sin fondo.
> (p. 471)

Now it is finished. Rain penetrates his mouth.
Like a madman the air flees his sunken chest,
and love, drenched in tears of snow,
warms itself on the top of the cattle ranches.

What are they saying? A stinking silence lies there.
We are before a dead body turning into air,
a clear form that once boasted nightingales
but now we see filling with bottomless holes.

Only his equals may mourn him—men who break horses and tame rivers. Their diluvial tears will compensate for the lack of water and carry away Ignacio's body to the other world.[22] There he will not hear the "double breathing of the bulls," for this ominous sound will be assimilated by the moon, the queen of all creatures, or it will disappear into the sea. In these stanzas every element of Lorca's mythology is majestically woven together:

> Que se pierda en la plaza redonda de la luna
> que finge cuando niña doliente res inmóvil;
> que se pierda en la noche sin canto de los peces
> y en la maleza blanca del humo congelado.
>
> No quiero que le tapen la cara con pañuelos
> para que se acostumbre con la muerte que lleva.
> Vete, Ignacio: No sientas el caliente bramido.
> Duerme, vuela, reposa: ¡También se muere el mar!
>
> (p. 472)

> Let it be lost in the round plaza of the moon,
> that pretends when a child to be a still and suffering beast;
> let it be lost in the songless night of the fish
> and in the white thicket of congealed smoke.
>
> I do not want them to cover his face with cloths
> so he may grow used to the death he bears.
> Go, Ignacio: Do not heed the hot bellowing.
> Dream, fly, repose: The sea also dies!

22. Correa reminds us that in primitive belief water was needed to carry the body of the victim to survival in the next world. Once again Lorca responded to mythical archetypes. The stone itself would represent the sacrificial altar as well as the slab upon which the victim lies in his niche (*La poesía mítica*, p. 109).

*Part 4:* "The Absent Soul" ("Alma ausente"). While the presence of the dead body was overwhelming, the memory of the spirit is fragile and evanescent. With the passage of time, Ignacio, like all the dead of the earth, will be unknown and forgotten. Not even his old adversary will know him, nor the stone upon which he lies:

> No te conoce el toro ni la higuera,
> ni caballos ni hormigas de tu casa.
> No te conoce el niño ni la tarde
> porque te has muerto para siempre.
>
> No te conoce el lomo de la piedra,
> ni el raso negro donde te destrozas.
> No te conoce tu recuerdo mudo
> porque te has muerto para siempre.
>
> El otoño vendrá con caracolas,
> uva de niebla y montes agrupados,
> pero nadie querrá mirar tus ojos
> porque te has muerto para siempre.
>
> (p. 472)

> The bull and the fig tree know you not,
> nor the horses and ants in your house.
> The child and the afternoon know you not
> because you have died forever.
>
> The back of the stone knows you not,
> nor the black satin where you decay.
> Your mute memory knows you not
> because you have died forever.
>
> Autumn will come with shells,
> misty grapes, and huddled hills,
> but no one will look into your eyes
> because you have died forever.

But still there is song; in the vital act of expression, Ignacio lives again:

> No te conoce nadie. No. Pero yo te canto.
> Yo canto para luego tu perfil y tu gracia.
> La madurez insigne de tu conocimiento.
> Tu apetencia de muerte y el gusto de su boca.
> La tristeza que tuvo tu valiente alegría.

Tardará mucho tiempo en nacer, si es que nace,
un andaluz tan claro, tan rico de aventura.
Yo canto su elegancia con palabras que gimen
y recuerdo una brisa triste por los olivos.

                                                    (p. 473)

No one knows you. But I shall sing of you.
Sing for posterity of your profile and your grace.
The famous wisdom of your skill.
Your appetite for death and the taste of its mouth.
The sadness that was present in your brave gaiety.

Much time will pass before there is born, if ever,
an Andalusian so noble, so rich in adventure.
I sing his elegance with words that wail,
and remember a sad breeze in the olive groves.

In his gypsy ballads, Lorca wove the life of primitive
people into a subconscious, mythical web. In mourning the
death of his friend, he attempted to express personal grief on
the same level. His response to death in terms of ancient symbols restored the primeval and somehow dignified kinship between man and the earth that had been sorely absent in his
New York poetry.

# Final Poems

". . . boundary of flesh and dream. . . ." (p. 501)

### ARABIC FORMS

Lorca's acquaintance with Arabic poetry written in Spain
during the Moorish occupation was secondhand.[23] Nevertheless, he always suspected that part of his wizardry at metaphor was related to Andalusia's oriental past, and, when he
returned to Spain from America, he began to compose a series of

23. In his lecture on the *cante jondo* in 1922, he referred (*Obras completas*,
p. 1529) to the "Asiatic poems" translated by Gaspar María de Nava in 1838 from
English and Latin versions, a very secondhand source indeed. Then in 1930
appeared the first edition of *Poemas arábigoandaluces* by Emilio García Gómez,
a collection of direct translations which may have figured as a partial inspiration for *Diván del Tamarit*.

poems in loose imitation of Arabic style. They were collected after his death and published in 1940.

Arabic-Andalusian poetry is of limited intellectual content, mainly descriptive, and bound by rigorous form. One of its chief attractions for Western readers has been its predominant sensuality, called by the scholar García Gómez a "frenzied adoration of physical beauty."[24] Lorca was drawn by both the sensuality and the extravagance of metaphor, for these poets of the African deserts and Andalusian sierras spent their genius in creating elaborate, mannered imagery that makes extended reading of their verse similar to passing through a labyrinth wrought by a tortured imagination. The rashness of their similes must have enthralled Lorca, who had already learned the art of exaggeration from Andalusian folklore; when he saw a threaded needle compared to a comet, oars to eyelashes, and eyebrows to a half-moon, he knew he was among his equals in relating the seemingly unrelated. The bathos of Arabic poetry, its exalted feelings about trivial things, would also have appealed to Lorca.

The following verse, written in the tenth century to a beautiful Moorish woman who had been partner to an all-night orgy, illustrates the quality of Arabic poetry to which Lorca responded:

> Su talle flexible era una rama que se balanceaba
> sobre el montón de arena de su cadera y de la que
> cogía mi corazón frutos de fuego.
>                              (García Gómez, p. 97)

> Her lithe waist was a branch swaying
> above the mound of sand of her hips, from which
> my heart gathered fiery fruit.

Lorca's habitual use of flowers as sexual images (see, for example, "Preciosa and the Wind") had its counterpart in much Hispano-Arabic verse, as witness this song written by Al-Mu'-tamid in the eleventh century:

---

24. *Poemas arábigoandaluces,* 4th ed. (Madrid: Espasa-Calpe, 1959), p. 48.

> She loosed her robe, that I might see
> her body lissom as a tree:
> the calyx opened in that hour
> and oh, the beauty of the flower.[25]

*Divan at the Tamarit* is a recognition of this atavistic debt: poems lightly masked in the Arabic forms of the *gacela* and the *casida,* between which Lorca apparently made no distinction. During the period of their composition, the main part of his energy went into the writing of plays, and, as has been suggested, we have no great poetry from these years. If *Divan at the Tamarit* is a reliable indication, Lorca's conscious efforts to cultivate the Arabic vein came to naught. The projected book, in the form it has reached us, adds nothing new, and some of the imagery seems especially forced, proving, in a poet like Lorca, that his inspiration was actively engaged elsewhere. Many poems recall earlier compositions—the *grito* of Andalusia still covers everything, now in the form of weeping:

> las lágrimas amordazan el viento,
> y no se oye otra cosa que el llanto.
>
> (p. 497)

> tears muzzle the wind,
> and nothing is heard but weeping.

As before, cosmic movements become human. The appearance in his poetry of a new animal may be due to his New York experience:

> Sentados con el agua en las rodillas
> dos valles esperaban al otoño.
> La penumbra con paso de elefante
> empujaba las ramas y los troncos.
>
> (p. 498)

> Seated with water in their laps,
> two valleys wait for autumn.
> The half-light with elephant tread
> pushes branches and tree trunks.

25. Ibn Sa'íd, 'Alī Mūsā, *Moorish Poetry,* trans. A. J. Arberry (Cambridge: Cambridge University Press, 1953), p. 1.

"The *Gacela* of Unforeseen Love" perpetuates his use of
flowers as sex symbols:

> Nadie comprendía el perfume
> de la oscura magnolia de tu vientre.
> Nadie sabía que martirizabas
> un colibrí de amor entre los dientes.
>
> Mil caballitos persas se dormían
> en la plaza con luna de tu frente,
> mientras que yo enlazaba cuatro noches
> tu cintura, enemiga de la nieve.
>
> (p. 485)

> No one understood the perfume
> of the dark magnolia on your belly.
> No one knew that you martyred
> a hummingbird of love between your teeth.
>
> A thousand Persian horses slept
> in the moonlit plaza of your forehead,
> while I four nights enwrapped
> your waist, the enemy of snow.

The comparison of the tongue to a hummingbird is worthy of
any poet of the caliphate of Córdoba, and the metaphor of the
whiteness of the waist recalls Góngora himself. But notwith-
standing, these poems lack the old spark, and many of them
are still struggling with the contrary heritage of *Poet in New
York.*

When Lorca forgets the translations of García Gómez, however, and remembers the Andalusian popular ballads, which
he knew by heart and which infiltrated so much of his work,
he achieves those delightful moments of which he alone was
capable:

> Gacela del mercado matutino
>
> > Por el arco de Elvira
> > quiero verte pasar,
> > para saber tu nombre
> > y ponerme a llorar.
>
> .    .    .    .    .

Por el arco de Elvira
voy a verte pasar,
para sentir tus muslos
y ponerme a llorar.

(p. 495)

*Gacela* of the Morning Market

By the arch of Elvira
I want to see you pass,
so I may learn your name
and begin to weep.

.    .    .    .    .

By the arch of Elvira
I go to watch you pass,
so I may see your thighs
and begin to weep.

Underneath Lorca's fabulous exuberance, there was a lonely man. This began to be apparent in New York and might have developed into a major theme had not the fateful appointment in Granada intervened. The "*Casida* of the Impossible Hand" shows a desire for stability in a world of swirling and violent impressions. He begs for a sustaining hand, a wounded one if possible, implying a need for shared sensitivity and suffering— something with which to blot out the baleful face of the moon, and to give substance to a life as fitful as dead leaves:

Yo no quiero más que una mano,
una mano herida, si es posible.
Yo no quiero más que una mano,
aunque pase mil noches sin lecho.

Sería un pálido lirio de cal,
sería una paloma amarrada a mi corazón,
sería el guardián que en la noche de mi tránsito
prohibiera en absoluto la entrada a la luna.

.    .    .    .    .    .    .    .

Lo demás todo pasa.
Rubor sin nombre ya, astro perpetuo.
Lo demás es lo otro; viento triste,
mientras las hojas huyen en bandadas.

(p. 500)

I want nothing more than a hand,
a wounded hand, if possible.
I want nothing more than a hand,
even though I spend a thousand nights without bed.

It would be a pale lily of lime,
it would be a dove moored to my heart,
it would be the watchman who the night of my transit
would resolutely forbid entrance to the moon.

.     .     .     .     .     .     .     .     .

The rest all passes.
A blush without name, perpetual star.
The rest is foreign; a sad wind,
While leaves flee in bands.

### THE WOUND OF LOVE

Death cut short the development of a series of poems pro-
visionally entitled "Sonnets of Dark Love." The four examples
we have in the collected works give a tantalizing glimpse of
Lorca approaching middle age, possessed by the usual strange
stirrings, and preoccupied by a need for form and measurement.

As he mused, free from the violent repulsion of previous
works, on the nature of death, he saw himself gathered into
the silence of the earth, symbolized by moss, stiffened doves, and
the inert branch. The "pulse of his style," his need to communicate, will be checked forever in an unreflecting "chaste
mirror." The mythical images are latent but not vital in these
final poems. Instead, he seems to have been working towards a
new manifestation of the synthesis between man and his natural environment. Somehow the silent branch and withering
flowers will retain a drop of his essence:

Yo sé que mi perfil será tranquilo
en el musgo de un norte sin reflejo.
Mercurio de vigilia, casto espejo
donde se quiebra el pulso de mi estilo.

Que si la yedra y el frescor del hilo
fue la norma del cuerpo que yo dejo,
mi perfil en la arena será un viejo
silencio sin rubor de cocodrilo.

Y aunque nunca tendrá sabor de llama
mi lengua de palomas ateridas
sino desierto gusto de retama,

libre signo de normas oprimidas
seré en el cuerpo de la yerta rama
y en el sinfín de dalias doloridas.

(p. 544–45)

I know that my profile will be tranquil
in the moss of an unreflecting north.
Mercury of vigil, a chaste mirror
where the pulse of my style is broken.

That if ivy and the freshness of thread
were the norm of the body I am leaving,
my profile in the sand will be an old
silence without the crocodile's blush.

And although my tongue of stiffened doves
will never have the taste of flame
but only the desert flavor of *genista,*

free sign of oppressed norms
I shall be in the body of the inert branch
and in the endlessness of suffering dahlias.

Yet the subject of these sonnets was to be love, a dark love like Shakespeare's, providing, as does all love, its share of suffering. Associating himself with the image of the tree, as he had done long ago in his first book of poems, he mourns the vital sap withheld by the loved one:

Tengo miedo a perder la maravilla
de tus ojos de estatua, y el acento
que de noche me pone en la mejilla
la solitaria rosa de tu aliento.

Tengo pena de ser en esta orilla
tronco sin ramas; y lo que más siento
es no tener la flor, pulpa o arcilla,
para el gusano de mi sufrimiento.

Si tú eres el tesoro oculto mío,
si eres mi cruz y mi dolor mojado,
si soy el perro de tu señorío,

no me dejes perder lo que he ganado
y decora las aguas de tu río
con hojas de mi otoño enajenado.

(p. 546)

I fear to lose the marvel
of your statue-like eyes, and the accent
placed at night upon my cheek
by the solitary flower of your breath.

I grieve to be upon this bank
a trunk minus branches; and even more I feel
the lack of flower, fruit, or clay,
on which to feed my worm of suffering.

If you are my obscure treasure,
if you are my cross and damp grief,
if I am the dog of your lordliness,

then let me not lose what I have won,
and decorate the waters of your river
with leaves from my enraptured autumn.

The note of tenderness and skillful control show that Lorca's search for new roots might have been amply rewarded. Yet it is idle to speculate. His profile is clear and strong as it stands. His generous vitality still overflows. An Andalusian so "rich in adventure" will not be born again for some time.

# The Dark Root of the Cry

TWO years before the publication of the *Gypsy Ballad-Book,* Lorca wrote to his friend Jorge Guillén, "The poem has still not been made that pierces the heart like a sword" (p. 1572). This observation points up Lorca's own goal in writing poetry, and, although he seems to be deploring to Guillén the difficulty of ever attaining such an end, many of his best lines have the sharp physical impact that was described by A. E. Housman as the basis of the poetic effect:

Experience has taught me, when I am shaving of a morning, to keep watch over my thoughts, because if a line of poetry

strays into my memory, my skin bristles so that the razor
ceases to act. This particular symptom is accompanied by
a shiver down the spine; there is another which consists
in a constriction of the throat and a precipitation of
water to the eyes; and there is a third which I can only
describe by borrowing a phrase from one of Keats's last
letters, where he says, speaking of Fanny Brawne, "everything that reminds me of her goes through me like a spear."[26]

Lorca's deep commitment to the idea that poetry should pen-
etrate the vitals of the reader can best be appreciated in his
lecture "Theory and Function of the *Duende*," which he composed in Cuba in 1930. It is a document important for a
thorough understanding of his work. *Duende* means hobgoblin,
but whenever the speaker wants to characterize something as
deeply stirring and dramatic, he says, "Esto tiene mucho
duende." A flamenco singer who has roused his listeners, or
a bullfighter who has made a perfect kill, will elicit the phrase,
spoken with respect and awe.

Aware of this common usage throughout Spain, Lorca elaborated the word *duende* to encompass the primitive, daemonic
source of artistic inspiration. The tremendous emotional impact
of the *cante jondo,* he said, could only be attributed to "dark
sounds" (*sonidos negros*) which are inspired not by the gentle
classical muse but by the *duende,* the spirit of the earth. The
*duende* wells up from the deepest quarters of the blood and
takes hold of the artist as he is creating. It responds most readily to music, dance, and spoken poetry, because a warm and
living body is needed for it to make its presence felt.

As a young man in 1918, Lorca described the effect upon
him of dogs ("those beings of unknown mythology") howling at night near a monastery. "There is something . . . in the
howl of a dog which fills us with fear. Without knowing what
kind of an emotion is possessing us, we can only understand

26. Quoted in Joseph Campbell, *The Masks of God: Primitive Mythology*
(New York: Viking, 1959), p. 41. Robert Graves makes use of the Housman
quote as the starting point for his own ideas about the physical impact of poetry
in *The White Goddess.*

that the sound is not made by the animal. We can only believe that a supernatural spirit is locked within those fearfully musical waverings that presage the latent anguish of the world . . ." (p. 1467). The emotion is the age-old spirit of terror and wonder that man has always felt in the face of the universe, and that is the stuff of myth and art. By 1930 the sophisticated author of the *Gypsy Ballad-Book* had recognized this fact: "These dark sounds are mystery, the roots reaching into the mud we all know and all ignore, but from which we derive what is real in art" (p. 37).

One need think only of the roll of drums, the blare of trumpets, or the wail of a siren to realize that the response to such sounds is universal. Lorca, in fact, seems to have adumbrated the Jungian idea of the archetype—that hidden form or image sleeping in the blood that is quickly released by certain objects, sounds, or works of art. Lorca, of course, knew nothing of Jung, but he was well aware, as his description of the wailing dogs reveals, that there are terrors which date beyond body, and that there are subjectively known forms which art, since its origins, has communicated by intuition, or, as he put it more poetically, by means of the "mirrors of the stars" (p. 1527). In his poetry he tried to evoke such images as much as possible. His lecture on the *duende* lists a series of objects that to him ultimately suggested death, and whether or not each one connotes a similar feeling for every reader, the implication is, as Jung declared, that these forms call forth from the unconscious a reaction that is shared by mankind: "The knife, the cart wheel, the razor, the prickly beards of shepherds, the peeled moon, the fly, damp cupboards, rubble, lace-covered icons, lime, the sharp line of eaves and balconies—these things have tiny bits of death in them, allusions and voices that to an alert mind summon up in our memory the cold sense of our final journey" (p. 43).

Among the many instances in Lorca's poetry that reveal the presence of the *duende,* we may recall, from "Lament for Ignacio Sánchez Mejías," these four suggestive lines that describe the moment just before the horns pierce Ignacio's groin:

> No se cerraron sus ojos
> cuando vio los cuernos cerca,
> pero las madres terribles
> levantaron la cabeza.
>
> (p. 468)
>
> His eyes did not close
> when he saw the horns near,
> but the terrible mothers
> raised their heads.

Upon first reading the phrase "las madres terribles," an uncanny feeling overcame me, and subsequent readings have always produced a shudder similar to the effect upon Housman of those stray lines of poetry that made the stubble of his chin bristle. The Terrible Mother has left numerous traces in mythology—her voracious maw was the jaws of death in which men were crunched to pieces. Horace evoked her as the *Mater saeva cupidium.* She is the wild, raging woman who determines the fate of Siegfried, and the Mithraic killing of the bull was a sacrifice to her.[27] And now at the moment when the hero Ignacio is about to die, she reappears. Lorca probably knew nothing about these mythological details, but the *duende* was present, and the phrase provokes from the reader a response that is explained at least in part by Jung's theories.

If we recognize Lorca's lecture on the *duende* as a statement concerning his own art, we can view his work in a new perspective that will explain much that has been dismissed as sheer whimsy, playfulness, or even perversion. Playfulness it is, but at the level of mythological creation. Studies have shown that Lorca's most common metaphor is one in which everything intermingles, in which the most antagonistic elements are related to each other, and it has been concluded that he had an eye for synthesis and analogy.[28] But primitive myth demonstrates that early man did not view the world with an analytical eye, separating things into cause and effect; rather, the im-

27. C. G. Jung, *Symbols of Transformation* (London: Routledge & Kegan Paul, 1956), pp. 389, 432.
28. Concha Zardoya, "La técnica metafórica de Federico García Lorca," *Revista Hispánica Moderna,* XX (1954), 311–14.

pulse behind myth seems to have been to underscore, in Cassirer's phrase, "the consanguinity of all things." Referring to the "dark sounds" that accompany the *duende,* Lorca pointed out that behind them ". . . lie in tender intimacy volcanoes, ants, soft breezes, and the great night clasping the milky way to its waist" (p. 47). The urge to proclaim this "tender intimacy" accounts for hundreds of his apparently bizarre metaphors:

> En el jazmín un elefante y nubes
> y en el toro el esqueleto de la niña.
>
> (p. 499)
>
> In the jasmine, an elephant and clouds,
> and in the bull, a small girl's skeleton.

According to the creation myth in West Ceram (the next major island westward of New Guinea), mankind emerged from a cluster of bananas.[29] Lorca's vision of a small girl's skeleton in the bull is "strange," therefore, only to our non-mythic orientation, our rational atomization of reality. Lorca's violent reaction to New York may have been due to an awareness that industrial civilization had made the world a duller place in terms of the imagination. His instructions to Stanton, the son of a farmer in Newburg, New York, show clearly that he believed there was a language of primitive relationships forgotten by modern man:

> Stanton, vete al bosque con tus arpas judías,
> vete para aprender celestiales palabras
> que duermen en los troncos, en nubes, en tortugas,
> en los perros dormidos, en el plomo, en el viento,
> en lirios que no duermen, en aguas que no copian,
> para que aprendas, hijo, lo que tu pueblo olvida.
>
> (p. 431)
>
> Stanton, go to the forest with your jew's-harp,
> go in order to learn celestial words
> asleep in trunks, in clouds, in turtles,
> in drowsing dogs, in lead, in the wind,
> in wakeful lilies, in waters that do not imitate,
> so that you may learn, my son, what your people forget.

29. Campbell, *Primitive Mythology,* p. 173.

## The Rites of Love and Death

The constant association of sex with violence is one of the most arresting notes in all of Lorca's work. Rarely does he celebrate the act of love as sensuous rapture or delightful physical intimacy; instead love is presented as a ruthless force that cruelly bends the will of his protagonists. In the play *Blood Wedding,* Leonardo justifies his adulterous love for the bride in these terms:

> Que yo no tengo la culpa,
> que la culpa es de la tierra
> y de ese olor que te sale
> de los pechos y las trenzas.
> (p. 1168)

> The fault is not mine,
> the fault is of the earth
> and that odor that comes from
> your breasts and your braids.

As Lorca's creatures succumb to this telluric force, the cosmic commotion that attends all of man's acts in his poetry increases in vigor. Preciosa fleeing the man-wind arouses the sympathy of the sea, which frowns and murmurs; after the gypsy has seduced the faithless wife, swords of lilies beat the air (p. 363). The martyrdom of St. Eulalia (pp. 386–88) is frankly presented in sexual terms, opening with a horse prancing through the streets of Mérida; during the barbarities committed upon the saint's flesh, her sex trembles like a bird caught in the brambles and she reels in a confused passion of manes and swords.

Every kind of sexual encounter, whether mythical or mundane, is accompanied by these portents, and frequently results in death. The barren wife in the drama *Yerma* kills her husband in the last scene, rolling on the ground with him in a grim parody of love-making. In the "Ballad of the Moon," death disguised as the moon-woman shows her breasts of slippery tin before she begins her dance of death in front of the boy. In the tender, bawdy, and farcical comedy, *The Love of Don Perlimplín for Belisa in His Garden,* the old man Perlimplín's triumph is to make the young and erotic Belisa fall in love with him, although it means his death.

A brief poem from *Songs,* called "Lucía Martínez," has this revealing stanza:

> Tus muslos como la tarde
> van de la luz a la sombra.
> Los azabaches recónditos
> oscurecen tus magnolias.
> (p. 326)

> Your thighs like the afternoon
> go from light to shadow.
> A hidden jewel of jet
> darkens your magnolias.

The movement towards the vital point of Lucía Martínez is from light to darkness, and jet (her sex) obscures the whiteness (magnolias) of her flesh. Thus we have at the center of sex a darkness and mystery, entered into from the light of day. Man, when he plunges into this darkness, may be renewing himself, but there are attendant dangers, as is made abundantly clear in *Poet in New York:*

> El amor está en las carnes desgarradas por la sed,
> en la choza diminuta que lucha con la inundación;
> el amor está en los fosos donde luchan las sierpes del hambre,
> en el triste mar que mece los cadáveres de las gaviotas
> y en el oscurísimo beso punzante debajo de las almohadas.
> (p. 449)

> Love is in flesh clawed by thirst,
> in a tiny hut fighting the flood;
> love is in the pits where hunger's serpents twist,
> in the sad sea where seagulls' bodies rock,
> and in the deep, dark pricking kiss underneath the pillow.

The list of passages demonstrating this alliance between love and disaster and death is so extensive that it demands more than a curt dismissal as some kind of morbid perversity on

Lorca's part. If we keep in mind the *duende*, the muse of the earth, and Lorca's constant reference to myth, we can uncover a highly suggestive explanation for this striking contiguity of sex and violence. We should not limit our investigation to Greek and Roman mythology, which Lorca knew, but rather move back in human culture to the love-death rituals of primitive agricultural societies. These rites he probably did not know, but the *duende* has mysterious ways of communication, as Lorca was fond of pointing out.

Constantly evolving in the sight of primitive man was the example of nature's yearly cycle: impregnation of the ground, flowering, harvest, and fallowness. Through myths, man attempted to come to terms with this impervious arrangement that provided life, sustained it, and then removed it. These myths explicitly unite creativity with death. In the culture of cannibal gardeners living on islands near New Guinea, the sexual organs are supposed to have appeared at the time of the coming of death into the world. In this same region, a chosen maid and man cohabit in view of the tribe, and are then lowered into a pit to be roasted and eaten. Fray Bernardino de Sahagún recorded the Aztec ceremony of the Maize Goddess, an annointed virgin who was beheaded and skinned, the clammy covering donned by the priests who had removed it. The implication is clear: these cruel deeds sanctify the bearing of fruit through death. "Reproduction without death would be a calamity, as would death without reproduction," notes Joseph Campbell, succinctly expressing the simple truth that lies behind such rites.[30]

Seen from this vantage point, Lorca's juxtaposing of love and death can be invested with the deep meaning of myth. He was reaching into the "mud we all know and all ignore." The dead men moaning under the naked woman's bed are awaiting their turn as part of the endless cycle of creativity and decay:

Casida de la mujer tendida

Verte desnuda es recordar la tierra.
La tierra lisa, limpia de caballos.

30. *Ibid.*, pp. 171, 177, 224.

La tierra sin un junco, forma pura
cerrada al porvenir: confín de plata.

Verte desnuda es comprender el ansia
de la lluvia que busca débil talle,
o la fiebre del mar de inmenso rostro
sin encontrar la luz de su mejilla.

La sangre sonará por las alcobas
y vendrá con espada fulgurante,
pero tú no sabrás dónde se ocultan
el corazón de sapo o la violeta.

Tu vientre es una lucha de raíces,
tus labios son un alba sin contorno,
bajo las rosas tibias de la cama
los muertos gimen esperando turno.

(pp. 498–99)

*Casida* of the Reclining Woman

To see you naked is to recall the earth.
The smooth earth, free of horses.
The earth without a reed, pure form
closed to the future: a silver restraint.

To see you naked is to understand the desire
of rain seeking a weak waist,
or the fever of the sea's huge face
unable to find the light of its cheek.

Blood will ring through the bedrooms
and arrive with gleaming sword,
but you will not know where are hidden
the toadish heart or the violet.

Your belly is a struggle of roots,
your lips a dawn without contour;
under the warm roses of your bed
the dead moan, awaiting their turn.

In the fall of 1960, a Lorca play (*Yerma*) was produced in Madrid for the first time since the flames of civil war enveloped Spain in 1936. It was so successful that it was repeated the following year. Thus one of the greatest masters of the Spanish language could finally be interpreted again on the Madrid stage. His poety, however, has long been known by heart wherever Spanish is spoken, and, like the culture of his native land, maintains a unique and immutable appeal. In the crucible of Andalusia, Lorca fused the passion of his race into moments of dark delight, which, kept alive by the *duende,* still rouse men's hearts in this impersonal, technological age.

### SELECTED WORKS
### OF GARCÍA LORCA
*(In order of composition)*

#### Poetry

*Libro de poemas* (1916–1920). Madrid: Maroto, 1921.
*Poema del cante jondo* (1921–1922). Madrid: CIAP, 1931.
*Canciones* (1921–1924). Málaga: Litoral, 1927.
*Primeras canciones* (1922). Madrid: Ed. Héroe, 1936.
*Romancero gitano* (1924–1927). Madrid: Revista de Occidente, 1928.
*Poeta en Nueva York* (1929–1930). Mexico City: Séneca, 1940.
"Diván del Tamarit" (1931–1936). *Revista Hispánica Moderna,* VI (1940), 307–11.
*Llanto por Ignacio Sánchez Mejías* (1934). Madrid: Cruz y Raya, 1935.
*Obras completas,* prólogo Jorge Guillén, epílogo Vicente Aleixandre, 4th ed. Madrid: Aguilar, 1960.

#### Theater

*(Dates in parentheses indicate first productions)*
*Bodas de sangre* (1933).
*Amor de don Perlimplín con Belisa en su jardín* (1933).
*Yerma* (1934).
*La casa de Bernarda Alba* (1945).

#### Lectures

"El cante jondo," Granada, 1922.
"La imagen poética de don Luis de Góngora," Granada, 1927.
"Teoría y juego del duende," Cuba, 1930.

### ENGLISH
### TRANSLATIONS

The pioneer effort and still one of the best English translations is that of Stephen Spender and J. L. Gili, *Poems* (New York: Oxford University Press, 1939). Since then Lorca has not lacked for translators. *Selected Poems,* ed. Francisco García Lorca and Donald M. Allen (Norfolk, Conn.: New Directions, 1955) is probably the best introduction. Facing the Spanish original are translations by such competent hands as Spender, Roy Campbell, Edwin Honig, Ben Belitt, Langston Hughes, Rolfe Humphries, Lysander Kemp, W. S. Merwin, William Jay Smith, and Harriet de Onís. This range of translating talent indicates the widespread interest in Lorca in the English-speaking world.

Rolfe Humphries spent over ten years on his translation of the *Romancero gitano* and, on the whole, he is eminently successful, especially in capturing the original Lorca rhythm: *The Gypsy Ballads of Federico García Lorca* (Bloomington: Indiana University Press, 1953).

Roy Campbell, whose dash paralleled Lorca's and whose personal experience of Spain was unique, has taken rather too much liberty. The English ballad hovers in the background, and his prudery is surprising: *Lorca: An Appreciation of His Poetry* (New Haven: Yale University Press, 1952).

Working from a typescript, often illegible, Rolfe Humphries produced the first English translation of *Poeta en Nueva York,* published in a bilingual edition (New York: Norton, 1940). A new translation upon a much emended text was done by Ben Belitt (New York: Grove Press, 1955). In a vigorous foreword, Mr. Belitt insists that the translator's task is twofold: he must first *translate out* of the foreign language and then *translate into* his native tongue. The result is arresting and on the whole impressive. It is only when one begins to poke a bit into the structure that the old and vexing question of liberty and treason returns again. But certainly Mr. Belitt has not been content with ". . . the self-serving complacencies of the 'accurate' way . . ." (p. xlii). This edition is especially valuable, furthermore, because it contains translations of Lorca's lectures on the *duende* and Góngora. The introduction by Angel del Río is a delicate balance of personal reminiscence and critical skill, suggesting the outlines which future study of this amazing book should follow.

Finally one cannot forget John Frederick Nims's excellent commentary and literal rendering in *The Poem Itself,* ed. Stanley Burnshaw (New York: Holt, 1960), pp. 232–51. For the even more literal minded there is *Lorca,* ed. J. L. Gili, with plain prose translations of each poem (London: Penguin Books, 1960). *An Anthology of Spanish Poetry,* ed. Angel Flores (New York: Anchor, 1961) has some new translations by Robert O'Brien and Rachel Benson. They are skillful, but the problem of retaining the magic of Lorca's *octosílabo* in the *Romancero gitano* still remains unsolved.

And finally, every reader should be reminded of Edwin Honig's

# INDEX

Aleixandre, Vicente, 140, 166
Alonso, Dámaso, 44n14, 69n26
Apuleius, Lucius, 169n15
Arabic-Andalusian poetry: influence of,
  on García Lorca, 198–200
Aragon, Louis, 190
Azaña, Manuel, 41
Azorín (pseudonym of José Martínez
  Ruiz), xviii, 59n19

Ballad. See Romance
Barnstone, Willis, 71–72, 134
Baroja, Pío, xviii, 44n13, 125
Baudelaire, Charles, 81
Bécquer, Gustavo Adolfo, influence of:
  on modern Spanish poetry, xvi, xxi;
  on Jiménez, xviii, 111; on Machado,
  36, 44, 44n14, 52–53
Belitt, Ben, 73, 184n19, 215
Benson, Rachel, 215
Bergson, Henri, 38; and Machado, 63–
  65
Blake, William, 79n2
Bly, Robert, 72
Brawne, Fanny, 206
Byron, George Gordon, Lord, xv

Caballero, Fernán, 162
Calderón de la Barca, Pedro, 52
Campbell, Roy, 215
Campoamor, Ramón de, xv
Camprubí Aymar, Zenobia, 116, 143;

marriage to Jiménez, 100–101, 105
Cante jondo, 140, 147, 151, 161; ori-
  gins, 152; García Lorca's treatment
  of, 152–60
Cantigas de amigo, xv
Carducci, Giosuè, 5
Cassirer, Ernst, 165, 166, 209
Castile: Unamuno exalts, 8–9; affects
  Machado, 37–39; as theme of Ma-
  chado's poetry, 58–63
Castro, Rosalía de, 36; influence on
  modern Spanish poetry, xv–xvi
Cela, Camilo José, 44
Cernuda, Luis, 6
Cervantes, Miguel de, xxii, 42, 52, 69
Cohen, J. M., 31, 134
Columbus, Christopher, 82, 143
Coplas, 46, 161–62
Correa, Gustavo, 157

Dalí, Salvador, 141
Dante Alighieri, 5
Darío, Rubén, 80; as modernista, xvi-
  xviii; and Machado, xvii, 35; and
  Unamuno, xviii, 6, 8; and Jiménez,
  82, 83. See also Modernismo
Death: preoccupation with, in Spain,
  xxii–xxiii; and García Lorca, xxiii;
  and Machado, xxiii, 66–67; and Jiménez, xxiii, 113; Unamuno obsessed with, 12–14, 27; Jiménez
  equates with life, 113–15; in García

Lorca, as part of gypsy life, 156–57; in García Lorca, associated with love, 210–13. *See also* Duende

Díaz-Plaja, Guillermo, 121

Dickinson, Emily, xvi

Donne, John, 114

Duende, 147, 212, 214; and poetry, 206–9; and death, 207; related to Jungian archetype, 207

Eliot, T. S., xxi, 139

Endymion, 169n15

Falla, Manuel de, 152

Flaubert, Gustave, xxii

Flores, Kate, 72, 134

Florit, Eugenio, 133, 134

Franco, Francisco, 43

Frank, Rachel, 134

Frazer, Sir James George, 165

Ganivet, Angel, xxii

García Gómez, Emilio, 199, 201

García Lorca, Federico, 137–216; influences on, xix; theories on poetry, xxi, 205–6; visual sense, xxii; personality of, 139–40; life, 139–45; *Poet in New York (Poeta en Nueva York)*, 142, 151, 180–91, 201, 211; *Gypsy Ballad-Book (Romancero gitano)*, 142, 164–80, 185, 188, 205, 207; as dramatist, 143; *The House of Bernarda Alba (La casa de Bernarda Alba)*, 143; *Blood Wedding (Bodas de sangre)*, 143, 180, 210; *Yerma*, 143, 210, 213; *Divan at the Tamarit (Diván del Tamarit)*, 144, 200–203; *Sonnets of Dark Love (Sonetos del amor oscuro)*, 144, 203–5; death of, 144–45; *Book of Poems (Libro de poemas)*, 145–52; imagery, logical clarity of, 147; symbol of sight, 149; and importance of song, 149–51; silence, 151, 155; myth, use of, 151–52, 164–66, 181–87, 208, 212–13; metaphor of *grito*, 154–55; *Poem of the Deep Song (Poema del cante jondo)*, 154–60; communication symbols, 157–58; *Songs (Canciones)*, 160–64, 211; moon as myth, 166–69, 173–79, 182; wind as myth, 169–73; sexual symbols, 179–80; tries to create a Negro myth, 183–86, 190; and surrealism, 190; and mythological significance of bullfighting, 191, 193; *Lament for Ignacio Sánchez Mejías (Llanto por Ignacio Sánchez Mejías)*, 191–98, 207–8; use of Arabic forms, 198–203; metaphor, synthetic nature of, 208–9; *The Love of Don Perlimplín for Belisa in His Garden (El amor de don Perlimplín por Belisa en su jardín)*, 211. *See also* Death, Duende, Love, Romance

Generation of '98, The, xviii

Gide, André, xxii

Gifford, Henry G., 73

Gili, J. L., 214, 215

God: Unamuno's concept of, 20–21; Machado's concept of, 67–68; Jiménez celebrates a personal god, 124–33

Goethe, Johann Wolfgang von, 107

Góngora, Luis de, 142, 201, 215

Goya, Francisco de, 8

Graves, Robert, 166, 194, 206n26

Greco, El, 124

Guillén, Jorge, 141, 164, 205

Gullón, Ricardo, 44n14, 79, 79n2, 99

Hays, H. R., 134

Heidegger, Martin, 69, 122

Honig, Edwin, 215–16

Horace, 208

Housman, A. E., 65n22, 208; theories on poetry, 53, 205–6

Howe, Julia, 134

Hughes, Langston, 215

Hugo, Victor, xv, xvii

Humphries, Rolfe, 215

Institución Libre de Enseñanza, 36, 41, 141

Jiménez, Juan Ramón, xvi, xxi, 75–135, 143; influence on García Lorca, xix, 160–61; theories on poetry, xxi, 79–80; impressionism, xxii, 91, 105; on Unamuno, 23n16; and Machado, 36, 38, 44n14; general character of his poetry, 77–82; *Tercera antolojía poética*, 78n1, 133; *Pastorales*, 80; *Violet Souls* (*Almas de violeta*), 80; *Water Lilies* (*Ninfeas*), 80; works, 80–82; *Laberinto*, 81; *Rock and Sky* (*Piedra y cielo*), 81; *Diary of Poet and Sea* (*Diario de poeta y mar*), 81, 82, 99, 101–7; *Animal of Depth* (*Animal de fondo*), 81, 82, 125–33; *Second Poetic Anthology* (*Segunda antolojía poética*), 81, 84, 100; *Spiritual Sonnets* (*Sonetos espirituales*), 81, 88; *Diary of a Newly Married Poet* (*Diario de un poeta recién casado*), 81, 101; *Poetry* (*in Verse*) (*Poesía* [*en verso*]), 81, 109, 113; *Beauty* (*in Verse*) (*Belleza* [*en verso*]), 81, 113; and mysticism, 81, 125, 128–33; *Platero and I* (*Platero y yo*), 81–82, 134; *Spaniards of Three Worlds* (*Españoles de tres mundos*), 82, 83; sadness and solitude, 83–84, 112; takes comfort in nature, 84–89; lack of identity, 89–91; *The Total Season* (*La estación total*), 95, 116–17; style, 97–99; marriage, 100–101; relationship between man and the world, 101, 118–23; effect of sea on, 101–7, 116; effect of travel on, 101–2, 118–19; *centro total*, 105, 117–18; *Eternities* (*Eternidades*), 107; preoccupation with language, 107–9; pantheism, 112; "Space" ("Espacio"), 119–21, 131–32; compared with García Lorca, 145. See also Death, God, Love, *Modernismo*, *Romance*

Jung, Carl, 207

Kazin, Alfred, 79n2
Keats, John, 206
Kemp, Lysander, 134, 215
Kerrigan, Anthony, 31
Kierkegaard, Søren, 3, 4

Leopardi, Giacomo, 5
Lévy-Bruhl, Lucien, 165
Lorca, Federico García. See García Lorca, Federico
Love: Jiménez' concepts of, 91–94; Jiménez relates to sea, 106; as theme in Jiménez, 128; and use of sexual symbols in García Lorca, 179–80; García Lorca associates with violence and death, 210–13

Machado, Antonio, 32–73, 82, 109, 141; influences García Lorca, xix; theories on poetry, xxi, 44–45; visual sense, xxii; life, 35–44; and Verlaine, 36, 83; objectivity versus subjectivity, 36–37, 41–43, 55–59; *Solitudes* (*Soledades*), 37, 44, 62, 64, 69; marriage, 37–39; *Fields of Castile* (*Campos de Castilla*), 38, 58–63, 69; Baeza, 39–40; Guiomar, 40–41; and Spanish Civil War, 41–44; Abel Martín and Juan de Mairena, 42, 68–69; on Marxism, 43; style, 44–52; water, as symbol, 46, 48, 54; plaza, as symbol, 50; symbolic meanings, 50–52; roads, as symbol, 50–54 *passim*; dreams, use of, 52–58, 64, 70; time, theme of, 63–66; philosophic poetry, 68–71; described by Jiménez, 113; compared to García Lorca, 145. See also Castile, Death, God, *Modernismo*, *Romance*
Machado, Manuel, 40
McVan, Alice Jane, 36n2, 72
Madariaga, Salvador de, 125
Maeztu, Ramiro de, xviii
Malinowski, Bronislaw, 165

Mallarmé, Stéphane, 5, 97, 103, 108, 111
Manrique, Jorge, 25, 67
Marías, Julián, xxiii, 20*n13*
Martínez Ruiz, José ("Azorín"), xviii, 59*n19*
Merwin, W. S., 134, 215
Milton, John, 5, 22, 96
*Modernismo:* Darío brings to Spain, xvii; and Jiménez, xvii, xviii, 78, 80, 82–83; Spanish reaction to, xviii; and Machado, xviii, 36; and Unamuno, 6, 7, 24. *See also* Darío
Moore, Marianne, 77
Al-Mu'tamid, 199

Nims, John Frederick, 215
Núñez de Arce, Gaspar, xv

O'Brien, Robert, 215
Onís, Harriet de, 215
Ortega y Gasset, José, xxi, 30, 56, 59*n19*
Otto, Rudolph, 130

Pascal, Blaise, 19
Pirandello, Luigi, 20
Primo de Rivera, Miguel, 24

Quevedo, Francisco de, 6

Residencia de Estudiantes, 141
Rexroth, Kenneth, 72
Rilke, Rainer Maria, xxiii
Río, Angel del, 142, 215
Ríos, Fernando de los, 142
Roach, Eloïse, 134–35
Rogers, Paul, 72
*Romance,* 81; form of, xix; influence on poets, xix; importance of, to Spanish poetry, xix, 161
Romanticism in Spain, xv

Sahagún, Fray Bernardino de, 212
St. Ignatius de Loyola, xxii

St. John of the Cross, xviii, xxi, 111, 124; compared to Jiménez, 128–29
Sánchez Barbudo, A., 20*n13*, 130
Santa Teresa de Jesús, 53, 124
Santayana, George, 52
Sartre, Jean-Paul, 20, 77, 79
Scott, Sir Walter, xv
Shakespeare, William, 42, 204
Silesius, Angelus, 21
Smith, William Jay, 215
Southey, Robert, xv
Spanish temperament, xx–xxiii
Spender, Stephen, 215

Tennyson, Alfred, Lord, 5
Thomas, Dylan, 139, 151
Tolstoy, Leo, 43*n9*
Tomlinson, Charles, 72–73
Trend, J. B., 72, 134
Turnbull, Eleanor L., 31, 72, 134

Unamuno, Miguel de, 3–31, 70, 115; and Darío, xviii, 6, 8; poetry *vs.* intellect, xxi, 4; importance as poet, 3, 6; sense of anguish, 3, 5; literary tastes, 5; need to stand out, 5; *Poesías,* 5, 6, 7, 18, 24; *The Christ of Velázquez (El Cristo de Velázquez),* 5, 7, 21–24; ideas on poetry, 6–8, 18; sonnet form, 7, 24; style, 7; stone imagery, 9–12; *Peace in War (Paz en la guerra),* 14; *Rosary of Lyric Sonnets (Rosario de sonetos líricos),* 14; contemplative, 14–15; religious struggle, 16–23 *passim,* 25–27, 29–30; conception of immortality, 17, 30; *The Life of Don Quixote and Sancho,* 18; struggle as affirmation of self, 18–19; *Mist (Niebla),* 20; *Ballads in Exile (Romancero del destierro),* 24; *From Fuerteventura to Paris (De Fuerteventura a París),* 24; *Song Book (Cancionero),* 24, 27–30; effect of exile on poetry, 24–27; theme of sea, 25–27; and Machado, 36, 37, 43*n9,*

# Index

223

67; *The Tragic Sense of Life,* 67. *See also* Castile, Death, God, *Modernismo, Romance*

Valéry, Paul, xviii, 103, 139; theories on poetry, 108, 109
Velázquez, Diego, xvii, 8, 31; inspires Unamuno, 21–23
Verlaine, Paul, xvii, 5, 6, 36, 44, 44*n14,* 46, 83

Villaespesa, Francisco, 83
Whitman, Walt, 189
Wilbur, Richard, 77
Wordsworth, William, 78

Yeats, William Butler, 78, 132, 143

Zardoya, Concha, 129
Zea, Carlos de Francisco, 134
Zorrilla, José, xv